MW01297129

Christmas Stories For The Horse Lover

Cynthia Seng

authorHOUSE®

AuthorHouse™
1663 Liberty Drive
Bloomington, IN 47403
www.authorhouse.com
Phone: 1-800-839-8640

First published by AuthorHouse 9/14/2011

ISBN: 978-1-4634-1181-7 (sc)

Library of Congress Control Number: 2011907929

Printed in the United States of America

Any people depicted in stock imagery provided by Thinkstock are models, and such images are being used for illustrative purposes only. Certain stock imagery © Thinkstock.

This book is printed on acid-free paper.

This book is dedicated to my husband Bill,
to my three wonderful children,
and to all of the horses I have known and loved.

Contents

Author's Note

Growing up on the outskirts of Chicago in the fifties and sixties, I could only dream of one day owning a horse. To compensate for this terrible circumstance, I did everything imaginable in my childish power to enrich my life with horses—without actually living within twenty miles of one. I made horses out of clay, and I made horses out of paper; I made horses out of snow and I found horses in the clouds. I eagerly read every book at the library on horses—I even had my very own riding stable business in the basement, next to the old coal hole and complete with saddled sawhorses and guest book. I cantered like a wild pony, my long mane lashing out in the wind, for I loved to run in my imaginary fields of green.

Over and over I would lasso the lamppost beyond our brownstone's cement stairs. I saved the nickel deposits on the glass Coke bottles in order to visit the little hobby shop in town that carried Breyer horses, shopping for the newest and brightest statue to add to my herd. I made tack from faux-leather strapping and fastened it with bent staples. I kept my corral of cowboys and ponies next to the bathtub and placed real grass (with real bugs, unfortunately) in the bottom of my nightstand for my little plastic friends. I read stories by Will James and Marguerite Henry by flashlight after bedtime, and visions of riding down lush trails put me to sleep every night. I felt the cold steel of a bit in my mouth when I rigged up bridle and reins and placed it on my head, wishing I could be that wonderful animal that I dreamed for. Making reins of heavy string, I would tie them to the handlebars of my little blue Schwinn bike and, with a bit of practice, I learned to steer my sleek stallion, his mighty hooves thundering beneath my wheels on the sidewalk.

I painted horses and more horses— horses of impossible colors and horses of every description. There were unicorns and winged horses and wild bucking broncs. I knew the name of every horse on every show on television, and I was sure I would grow up to be a veterinarian. The jumping course I set up in the alley with old cans, lumber, and whatever else I could find while garbage-picking (a great pastime back then—little red wagon and all) was a constant source of summer fun. I made plans to build a life-sized mechanical horse that I could get on and ride, which, of course, never happened—but the thought gave me plenty of hours of wishful thinking. Oh, why hadn't I been born on a farm!

Passion is a strong emotion and, sure enough, the day came, when I was sixteen, that I bought my first horse. His name was Buddy Shank, and he was a registered quarter horse. If I try hard enough, I can close my eyes and remember—no, actually *feel*—the way I felt the day that he became mine. Buddy is long gone now, but my aged mare grazes just beyond my window as I type. She has given me thirty-two years of joy, and she remains strong and sound. The spirit, the beauty, and the mystery of this magnificent animal have given me more happiness in my life than anyone could hope for. Many years have gone by, and many horses have entered my life in all kinds of ways, yet these marvelous creatures continue to fascinate me at the palette, at the sculpting stand, and in the stories I weave.

I hope that in one or more of these stories I can convey that passion to you and make you laugh, smile, or even cry. If the horse is in your heart, you have found a great friend for life. God bless and good riding, even if it is only in your dreams.

Best wishes,
Cindy

Buster's Last Stand

*I*t was a Saturday afternoon deep in November, and I had just finished putting the final touches on the fancy little picket fence as my wife stood beaming in the doorway. "Oh, Bill!" she exclaimed, "It's just terrific—I love it!"

Well, she should, I thought grumpily as I stood there and smiled back. Four trips to the hardware store and two hundred and fifty bucks later, here I stood next to what should have taken half the time and about a third of the cost. *But,* I thought to myself, *She likes it!* It made me feel good to make something from nothing. It was similar, in fact, to our little home in the country which we'd had only a short time but which we'd poured a generous amount of time and care into. Even our kids loved the country life and while Jake puttered up and down the driveway on the old Ford tractor, Cassie burrowed into daydream upon daydream in which a horse magically appeared. Only my wife, Suzanne, at times missed the hustle and bustle and city sounds we'd left behind, although from the looks of the last few phone bills, she'd been keeping right up with the girls in the old neighborhood. Since the move had been my idea—and I was mostly chicken at heart—I kept my mouth shut. *What price sanity?* I asked myself—and found the answer in the checkbook under "Illinois Bell Telephone".

From a distance, I could hear Mr. Phillips, our postman, as he made midday stops along his route. At each mailbox, his shaky truck would explode in a fit of old age and cough up great, gassy belches as he started back up. I stood out in the roadway and caught our mail on the fly as Mr. Phillips bore down on the accelerator, leaving me and the mail in a cloud of fumes and dust. I picked out the weekly newspaper and went inside to read the local news and ads. It didn't take much time to get to the last page, and as I glanced down at the ads, there it was—the ad for the horse. It read:

> AQHA Gelding, 15h, well-mannered.
> Guaranteed sound.
> Best offer or will trade for equal value.

Hey, perfect! I circled the phone number and showed Suzanne the ad.

"Aqua, huh? Didn't know they came in pastels …" she said distractedly.

Oh boy, I thought to myself—*she really* is *a city girl.* But, then again, and since I didn't know a gelding from a mare—or a pony, for that matter—I figured I'd better call Gramps; at least he'd know how many *h*'s they were supposed to have and what sound they were guaranteed to make.

"Gramps," who was nearly eighty, had been a cavalry man in World War I and never once let you forget it. He had kept his interest in horses, and I guessed him to be a pretty good feller to call on for advice. "Gramps!" I shouted into the phone. "I need some help in getting a horse!"

"A divorce?" he roared back, "Give 'er some time, son, she'll come around!" After a few loud comments, we got on the same subject, and I could almost feel the glint in his eyes as he agreed to come out and look over the animal. We agreed on a time and hung up. Rubbing my ear, I looked out the window at Cassie, who was riding her bicycle in the frosty air, baler-twine reins tied to the handlebars, pumping up for a fine race across the field.

"It would really be a great family present, wouldn't it, Suzanne?" I asked as she bent over her African violets.

"Must be root rot," she replied, frowning. I was on my own.

The next day I picked up Gramps, who was toting a very severe-looking riding crop, and we set off to see the horse. It was only a few miles from our house, and as we pulled into the yard, I was full of expectation. Gramps gruffly tugged my sleeve and said sharply, "Settle down, boy; I'll handle the talkin'!" As we approached the barn, Gramps and the owner of the horse, Mr. Butz, were engaged in a most confusing dialog about gates, confirmation, and boat tendons. Each time Gramps would speak, he would accentuate his comment with a wide swing of the crop, which the fellow would duck. We stood in front of a large stall and looked in on Buster, the horse. Buster gave each of us a very thoughtful stare and went back to munching his hay. Gramps strode into the stall and began feeling the horse's legs and running his hands all over the horse's body, giving what looked to be a grand overall inspection. Buster was a perfect gentleman throughout his physical, and we learned that he was twelve years old, had been ridden by children, and would pull a cart, to boot. We thought it best to try him out, and as Gramps and I stamped our feet in the cold, Mr. Butz saddled the horse. Mr. Butz bridled Buster and was about to mount up when up charged Gramps, insisting upon riding the horse himself.

Mr. Butz gave me a very doubtful look, and I said, "Hey, Gramps, let's just see how he goes first, okay?" I was near pleading, as I didn't think the old man had been that high in the air since lightning had hit the house some years back and thrown him out of bed.

I turned to Mr. Butz to assure him that it wasn't necessary for Gramps to ride the horse, when, all of a sudden, Gramps had a foot in the stirrup. Buster took a good look at the crop, tore the reins out of Mr. Butz's hands, and off they went, gravel flying and Gramps hanging on to the side of the saddle. We ran after the pair as the last of Gramps' coattails disappeared around the side of the barn. I felt a sinking sensation as I slowed down and envisioned the funeral—they'd all be there, blaming me for dear old Dad's demise. Mr. Butz had a sick look on his face as well, thinking, I'm sure, of whether his insurance was paid up on the place. I began to say something cheerful about Grandad's expertise, and as Mr. Butz gave me a withering look we heard the sound of galloping hooves and a hearty "To victory!" as Gramps and Buster came flying around the bend. The old man's white hair was flat back, and his false teeth were bared to the charge. He was pointing his crop to the enemy and urging Buster on with every stride. Buster looked rather heroic himself, I decided, whites of the eyes showing, tail cutting the air, bit clenched firmly in his mouth. Before my heart could skip another beat, the horse decided to strategically end the ambush by making a perfect ninety-degree turn into the barn, and then he screeched to a blazing halt. Gramps, who had lost his crop, his eyeglasses, and nearly his life, extracted himself from the horse's neck and stood there straight as an arrow in front of the horse. He gave Buster a warm slap and saluted. By this time, Mr. Butz had lost all words and just stood there dumbfounded. Gramps was sold—we'd found our horse.

After a little bit of bartering, Mr. Butz agreed to trade the horse, the saddle, and an old bobsled and harness for a less-than-perfect riding lawnmower and eighty dollars. I figured I'd gotten the better part of the deal and a darned good Christmas present that would reap benefits in spring, when Buster would cut and fertilize the grass—more than the old mower could offer. Mr. Butz also agreed to keep Buster until Christmas Day, when we would bring him home over the road and surprise the kids.

December set in, with snow nearly every day. A colorful string of Christmas lights hung from the little white picket fence, and our country home took on a glow, nestled neatly in an ivory blanket, untouched by the exhaust and road grime so inevitable in town. Each day Mr. Philips would deliver the holiday cards and mail, always announcing his arrival from about a mile away. Inside, our Christmas tree was a delight, decorated in the old-fashioned country way, with cranberry and popcorn strings flanking its generous boughs—although each day a few less kernels of popcorn graced the greens. "Must be the house wren!" Suzanne would say merrily as she baked holiday cookies, and the kids stood munching with unbroken stares at the growing pile of gifts scattered beneath the tree.

"Ah, Christmas!" I'd exclaim, and we all felt the gladness of being together and in a warm and wonderful place that we loved. By the third week of December, I had fixed up one of the stalls in the elderly barn on our property and passed off the questioning remarks and curious visits of the children with the statement: "Oh, making room for some of the things we have to get out of the garage; want to help?" Since it looked like a lot of work, they scurried away, and soon it was just another project.

Christmas Eve arrived, and we were off to Aunt Edy's for dinner and celebration. I kept thinking about Buster and our trip the next day to pick him up. By golly, I think I was more excited than anybody could ever be over that horse! The kids begged to stay overnight, and Uncle Gerry promised to return them home the next day—it would be ideal. That evening, lying close to Suzanne in our wonderful feather bed, I dozed off with visions of Buster grazing busily on my manicured lawn—a picture of content dotted here and there with fertilizer.

Christmas morning dawned with steady, light snow, and as Suzanne and I dressed in our warmest clothing, I thought ahead to the glorious moment when we would come prancing homeward with Buster. Suzanne poured the steaming coffee and asked sleepily, "Do you think Santa got started this way?"

I stared at the pile of newly purchased horse gear and replied, "Well, if he did, I hope he got a quantity discount!"

Mr. Butz had Buster ready when we arrived at his farm, and we all agreed that he looked very dashing in his harness, the large sleigh bells jingling with his every move. Mr. Butz urged me to climb in beside him while he showed me how to maneuver the horse and sleigh in the snow-packed driveway. Buster came alive beneath the long reins, and we swept about the yard, bells ringing and our breaths steaming in the pure, crisp air. I felt I was ready when the terrified look left Mr. Butz's face, and he relaxed his death grip on the front seat. I waved to Suzanne, who stood shivering in the yard and who I could plainly see was beginning to lose enthusiasm for the project. Mr. Butz clambered out, Suzanne climbed into the seat next to me, and we wrapped the warm lap blanket around our legs as Mr. Butz gave us final directions and a small bit of advice. "Whatever you do, don't get him cantering; just let him trot out, and you'll be fine." I started to ask him what cantering was, but by then Buster was already moving out at a brisk jog toward the road. Mr. Butz carefully pocketed his cash and mentally did a sign of the cross as we left his drive.

Oh, what a feeling! By the time we were a mile or so from the house, we were singing Christmas carols and having the time of our lives. Buster kept time with each bob of his blinkers, and his tail brushed our laps. I was doing great, I thought, totally in control. It was a beautiful, calm morning, and not another sound could be heard over the crunch of snow and the musical tinkling of the bells bouncing along Buster's flanks. We were just a quarter of a mile away from home, when I heard the familiar sound of

Mr. Phillip's truck from somewhere behind us. "Surely he's not delivering mail today," I said as I looked over my shoulder at the approaching racket. I could see him in the distance, bearing down upon us as fine snow sprayed away from the decrepit vehicle. With each bounce of the wheels, the thing would backfire rebelliously, spouting a sooty trail in its wake. In growing agitation, Buster kept turning his head this way and that to catch a glimpse of what was coming to swallow him alive, and as I took one final look behind, he managed to tear the reins from my numbed hands in a dash for safety.

Suzanne slumped back into the seat, and her mittens covered her eyes. "Is he can-ter-ing?" she cried, and beneath us we could feel the sleigh began to creak and sway. I snatched the reins back and felt my hat leaving its warm perch. Buster was in his glory, galloping over the slick pavement with Mr. Phillips in hot pursuit. "If I could only see," I thought to myself as his thick tail wrapped itself around my face. Our home driveway came into view, and as I hauled back on the reins, the back of the rickety seat gave way. Suzanne and I tumbled backward into the body of the sleigh. Buster spotted the opening and put the brakes on, his hooves skidding over the snowy road as he prepared to make his well-practiced ninety-degree turn. As we skittered through the turn, I was able to catch a fleeting glimpse of Mr. Phillips as he roared on by, and we heard a muffled greeting from somewhere in the vicinity of the shrouded, snowblown truck. I heard the crunch as the white picket fence crumpled and splintered beneath the runners of the sleigh, and as we fought to regain our balance, I could see our children jumping up and down, clapping their hands and shouting with delight at our holiday spectacle. We hit the backyard, and Buster slowed down. He trotted right on into the barn as if he'd lived there his whole life, and he dropped his head at a bale of hay.

I peeked over the side of the sleigh and gingerly sat up. From beneath the rumpled lap blanket, I could see a pair of eyes looking back at me, and they weren't smiling. I helped Suzanne to her feet, and as she dropped over the side of the sleigh to the ground, she rubbed her rump and remarked testily, "Next time I'd appreciate it very much if you left me home!" I was searching for a few appropriate words, when the kids came running into the barn, fussing over Buster and chattering excitedly. "Is he really ours? What's his name? Can we have a ride?"

I looked over at Buster, who was draped with our outdoor Christmas lights. "Let me unplug him, first," I said. I was beginning to feel better. Uncle Gerry appeared in the barn, holding an envelope and clutching at his side, which was sore from laughing. "Here's a little something from the mailman," he chuckled, and he handed me a card with a horse and a sleigh on the front. The inside proclaimed the message, "Merry Christmas and Happy New Year," signed, Mr. Phillips.

Well, it's been a few years since that day, and I'm happy to report that Buster has been a great addition to our family. We have had many a fine day with him: riding, driving—he does it all, and he has been quite patient with us. Gramps visits from time to time, and I truly believe Buster draws himself up and regards Gramps as an old war buddy. The kids are happy, my lawn is kept neatly—by a new, used mower—and Buster has the back pasture all to himself. Somehow, he just doesn't seem to fancy that new picket fence.

Forever Runnin' Wild

Bundle up and cowboy down for a trip to Wolf Canyon ...

His telephone call came late on a Friday evening, right around the time that I was kicking off my worn leather boots. To be honest, I didn't know whether to be excited, worried, or just plain confused. The call was from my father in Arizona, and as I sat in the kaleidoscopic glow of the flickering fireplace light, he told me that he'd been thinking of going on a one-nighter in the mountains—just the two of us, that was—just as soon as I could get things ready. Dad was in his seventies—and a few hundred miles away, to boot—and here he was ordering me to pack it up, because we were packing it in—the very next day. As I was beginning to think his oats were toasted or he was just plain kidding around, he gave me one last directive. "And, son," he said, "I want Winchester. See you in the morning.' At that, I hung up and sat back to ponder, gazing into the changing flames and wondering how my elderly father and his equally aged horse were going to make the trip.

Winchester was a sorrel stallion that Dad had raised from a wild-eyed, snorty two-year-old. The horse got his name from the man who traded him to us for the price of a good used rifle. I think the fellow might have given his right leg to try out the new gun on the red stud—his left leg was in a fresh cast from his last disagreement with the ornery Winchester. Dad looked over his new horse standing there all goose-rumped and trembling. He remarked over and over what a fine animal he was, in spite of his reputation for hurting folks. As it turned out, Winchester was not only mean but he had a wicked intelligence, which provoked a lot of cussing, head-scratching, and practice bronc-riding for the cowboys at the ranch. One day, Dad had plainly gotten his fill, so he saddled up and ponied the red devil up into the hills. It was a week or so later that Dad came riding back in on the sorrel, who was acting very much like a respectable cow horse should. I never did find out what had gone on up in those mountains, but it must have made good sense to Winchester. He went on to be a top mount; he was sturdy and strong and afraid of nothing, the kind of horse who put out all he had and then some. He did not settle down, though, like a real good ranch horse, and most hands declined to use him, saying, "He's quite a pleasure horse—that is, a pleasure to get *off* of!" Dad was the only one who got along with him, so they made quite the familiar pair doing the daily chores necessary on our cattle ranch. We let Winchester run in the winter and early spring with a small band of good mares, and we raised up his colts year after year. When the rigors of time caught up with him, he was retired from his cowpony duties but allowed to remain in a kind of horse heaven—free to roam the sprawling acres with only the stiffness in his legs to hinder him.

As I drove to meet Dad's flight the next day, in the predawn dimness, I felt a growing excitement about our upcoming adventure, even though it was getting a bit late in the fall for an impromptu pack trip. And Dad may have been a bit long in the tooth, but he was still a capable rider, and I looked forward to seeing him again. The Colorado countryside was in its plain brown wrap for its winter's rest, and our brief snowfalls hadn't yet been able to cover the land that was stubborn in its determination to delay the impending winter. I pointed the pickup truck into the uncrowded airport and spotted his impatient frame at the curb, duffle bag in hand and looking very much as if he'd just stepped off the set of a John Wayne oldie. I grabbed his gloved hands in mine, and with a hearty greeting, I drew back to get a better look. He was dressed for the ride in woolen overclothes, heavy denim, and insulated boots, and his face beneath the dull, shapeless Stetson was as worn as the buckle at his waist. As we drove back to the ranch, we spoke of our lives as if we were exchanging fragments of a letter—catching up was never easy. Dad was "fine, yes, couldn't be better," yet I knew it was far from the truth. His once-ruddy complexion was pallid, and I watched his face as his gray eyes fed his hunger for the Colorado land that he had grown up on. He gazed deeply at landmarks that had passed without notice years ago when he ran the Northpine Ranch. Dad fell quiet, lost in his past, and I was happy to oblige him.

When we arrived at the ranch, he just sat there in the stilled truck and let his memory continue to play back the reels of pictures that ran through his head. It was a long time, it seemed, before he looked up to see my wife and kids spilling out of the house to greet him with great big hugs and all the news. "Chipper had her puppies last night, Grandpa! They're in the barn—come, I'll show you!"

"Dad, so good to see you! How about a cup of my famous coffee?"

"Can you take us practice shooting, Grandpa? Did you bring your gun? Can I help you get your horse ready?"

"Are you going to stay 'til Christmas, Grandpa? Please?"

Dad just grabbed heads and hands and laughed a good, deep-down laugh. He turned to get his bag, saying, "Well, maybe in a little while. Got some business to attend to for a day or so, but I'll bet you'll be able to hold down the old place and those pups until then." He had some trouble lifting his bag out of the bed of the truck, but as I came around to give him a hand he'd have none of it.

I sent two of the boys to saddle the horses and the other to retrieve the supplies I'd packed, which would sustain us during our chilly night in the mountains. Dad kept staring up at those peaks while we were readying the horses, and I thought it odd that he didn't care to make his customary inspection of the cattle in our pens. He grabbed a pole on the stock chute and looked down at the earth. "Put this pole in myself—twice," he said slowly. "One day we was trying to load the old bull, but he just came right on through, busted 'er clean in half, and I figgered he knew his days were numbered, because he dang near made it back out to his herd before we could get a rope on him. Wasn't nothin' wrong with him; he was just old—just too old to keep around. " He lifted his eyes, and I saw an extinguished expression deep inside like nothing I'd ever seen before on his lined face. My gut twisted up, and, with a whole lot of misgiving, I said, "Ready? Good. Son, bring that old, mean, lop-eared, three-legged horse over here for your grandfather. "

Once mounted, we headed off with a last wave of good-bye beneath the wooden sign with the big NP brand burned into it. We settled down for our half-day trek to a favorite spot we both enjoyed near Wolf Canyon. Wolf Canyon was a masterpiece of the wild, with a deep valley of virgin meadow that no man had ever put a post to or grazed his stock on. Impenetrable, formidable walls of rock flanked the scrub, and within the canyon's deep chasm lay a panorama of peaceful beauty that one could marvel at from the hoof-worn path above it. Legend claimed that it sheltered the souls of the brave, both man and beast. If one camped along its broad top line, one could hear the rustle of trodden grass and murmuring spirits, and campfire smoke would curl in mysterious spirals toward its basin. Dad truly respected that canyon in its magnitude and danger, perhaps regarding it as his personal refuge from the things in life that dampened his soul or crimped his ambitions.

Our first hour and a half on the trail were spent quietly, with the only real conversation coming from Canada, the pack mare, who hollered her discontent at leaving her weanling filly behind. About two hours into the trip, our border collie, Heeler, appeared in silent silhouette at my horse's heels, and I swore at him for tagging along. "Doggone you, pup—you belong at home! They'll be looking for you, but I s'pose they'll figure it out. You'll get sore feet, you ragtag dog!" Heeler was a third-generation border collie around our place, and Dad himself had picked out the dog's grandfather. Ironically enough, Heeler was a pretty close double for his grandpappy, and as I looked at Dad and Winchester and the dog, I felt like a little boy again, out on a hunting trip some thirty years back. I can't say that my Dad and I were always close, but we shared an unbridled eagerness for the land and the cattle and the horses. We exchanged mental notes and half-sentences, and we got into more than one heated argument over horse pedigrees, cattle management, and things like who made the best chili in town. One day we were getting hot under the collar and betting on who could run a fence line quicker, and, after working the whole day like a polecat in a henhouse, I'd realized that he'd gotten the better of me—again. Why, he had gotten two days' work for a day's wages, and it had only cost him a sawbuck. I smiled in remembrance of those times.

As the trail became steeper and rockier, we paused several times to rest the horses. A few more hours, and we arrived at our campsite: a pretty little clearing with sheltering trees and the burbling of a nearby mountain brook beckoning at the edge.

We made camp, and I cared for the horses, while Dad busied himself with the housekeeping end of things. When I returned from carrying in the kindling wood, I could see him hunched over his duffle bag, and I knew something wasn't right. I dropped my bundle and began to run toward him. As I scrambled over the provisions, he straightened somewhat, but the pain was in his face as he grabbed himself in a tight hug. "What is it? What's wrong?" I yelled. He garbled a broken phrase, and I felt helpless as he motioned me away and slowly began to loosen up. "I'll be fine," he whispered with a contorted grin and sat heavily back on the bedroll. I stood there with heart pounding and demanded an explanation. "A touch of mountain fever from an old stag," he said at long last. "Happens when I get doing things like riding these old broncs for too long and too far. After all these years, Winchester is getting his revenge." Relieved to see the color returning to his face, I turned back to my task, with concern for him taking hold and his pride holding me back.

We got a good fire going and had dinner ready in no time. The sun began its dutiful descent, and as it burned through the tree line, we sat stuffed and content as two old hound dogs on a Louisiana porch. We began to talk—long, rich talk—open talk that blended the generations into a colorful tapestry that we draped and shared between us as we sat cozily by the fire. We talked for hours, while Heeler curled up and snored peacefully a small distance from the open flames. The conversation dimmed, and, long after the twilight was snuffed, Dad pointed to a small pine sitting at the edge of the forest. "It'd make a dandy," he said. "Take it for your Christmas this year."

"Sure, Dad," I replied, smiling and thinking of how ridiculous it would be to pack that little pine five hours back to the house. Christmas was just a few short weeks away, and I lay there thinking of how nice it was to have most of my special shopping done—a new vest for Dad, Sharon's boots, new things for the kids.

As if he were reading my mind, Dad growled, "Hey, don't be buyin' me no presents for Christmas, son. Got me a truckload of fancy treasures right now you'll be havin' to burn one day. "

"All right, Dad," I said. "What if I just put that old coot of a horse of yours on a plane for you?"

Dad said that would be all right, but he wasn't "buyin' him no drinks or carryin' his luggage."

A few more moments passed, and as I looked up at the partially clear sky with the stars poking through, I murmured, "We got an awful lot to be glad of, don't we?"

His answer was a nod, and then he said he was going to turn in for the night. We took off our boots, burrowed deep into our bags, and said goodnight. "You've been a good son," he said after a while, and, in my dreamlike state, I mumbled a reply. It was the last time I would ever hear his voice.

I awoke, blinking, to find a good snowfall beginning to swirl about the campsite. As I became fully awake, I said, "Hey, we'd better get a move on; this stuff is for keeps!" I squirmed out of my bag and stood up to shake off—and found myself alone. Dad was gone. His bag lay neatly folded, and as my eyes struggled to see through the white, I could tell that Winchester was gone as well. My eyes searched the mountains for a sign but saw nothing. Apprehension began to churn within me, and my mind raced to think of where they might have gone. Instinctively, I looked to the north, toward Wolf Canyon and the rugged terrain beyond. As I hastily saddled my horse, I cut Canada her freedom, and she was swallowed by the storm and gone in an instant. I turned my reluctant mount into the wind and urged him on toward the canyon. We got as far as a pass, fighting the blasts of the storm, which was beginning to build in devilish intensity. I pushed on toward the canyon and as we struggled up its craggy path, I saw a form ahead. It was Heeler, tied to a short, stout branch protruding from the mountainside; he was cowering in the blinding snow and plainly glad to see me. I dismounted and set him free, and, when I looked ahead to the treacherous ledges, I knew it was foolish to persist in the face of the storm's icy rage. Concern for my father drove me on, and I went as far as I dared but found no trace of the pair. "He wagered and he won," I told myself, gritting my teeth in anger and frustration. I began my careful retreat, feeling not the sting of the snow at my back but the sharpness of fear and bewilderment. I spurred my horse on, leaving only fading hoofprints and the abandoned search behind.

When I made it down as far as our campsite, I gathered up what I could find. With one last look behind me, I saw in my mind the lone pine squatting there at the edge of the clearing. I hacked it down and towed it in the deepening drifts, lost in my thoughts and yet at a loss for anything to think about. I rode as far as an old line camp beyond the ridge and put up for the day. The storm was in its full glory, howling its delight about the cabin and busily banishing the downed leaves and vestige of the season past. Cold and shivering, I sat with only the brown pools of the dog's eyes on mine as we waited out the storm.

I was able to push on late in the next day, but the journey was lengthened by the many detours I had to make around chest-high drifts. I cut over to the highway and made it home past suppertime with only my empty hands and grim explanation to relieve my very worried family.

I went immediately to work organizing a search party, although passage in the mountains was nearly impossible, even with snowmobiles. I also made a call to Dad's closest friend, a man with whom Dad had shared most of his life and who might have understood and shed some light on Dad's escapade. Instead of expressing surprise or shock, he spoke quietly, "Your father was dying, Luke. He went to the only place where he thought he could find relief from what had finally fenced him in." He paused and then continued, "He's found it now. Be glad for him, and try to understand. He loved you all very much." After I got off the phone, I walked out of the house and into the clear, bitter air. I went over to the barn, where the small, battered pine tree lay all covered with snow. I slowly removed the lariat from it and as I looked up to the white-capped peaks above, I could see the image of my father and Winchester. I saw him sitting big on his damp, heaving horse counting the spring calves, and I saw him sitting at the kitchen table late at night making payroll, writing checks, and marking dates. And then I saw him smile. He was a cattleman, horseman, husband, and father, and I was at last able to see his story through. It was cold, but I felt no chill. My anger melted into a feeling of peace, his final gift to me.

We had a quiet Christmas but a good one that year, and our tree was a glowing monument to the memory of Dad. When I look to the mountains now, I know he and Winchester are up there somewhere, young and strong, herding cattle or running down strays. They're in their glory there, the two of them, feeling good and feeling free to explore the secrets of Wolf Canyon and that great cathedral beyond.

Momma's Very Best Christmas

Things don't always go the way we plan them …

We weren't brats, really, unless you wanted to believe Old Man Baldersip down the road—who had shaken us out of his wormy, nasty, miserable old apple tree on occasion. Why, he even came across as daffy to most grownups. We were just a couple of average kids growing up on a small dairy farm, which was pretty far from town if your only avenue of transportation was a pair of secondhand bicycles. And from the looks of ours, all they were good for was watching prissy Uncle Mike trip over them on a rush trip to the "half-moon palace," as we fondly called the outhouse in those days.

Our family had a small herd of registered Jersey milk cows, a dozen milking goats, a few dogs, and three horses that Momma had rescued after the Saint Francis people came and took them away from a family out of luck in the county. The horses were half-starved when they arrived, but after we bulked them up some, my brother Jimmy and I discovered a whole new form of transportation—and this time they had four legs and no blowouts! Jimmy and I—Sarah —are twins; we were just ten years old when the horses and new brother Bryon arrived, so, in those long months when Momma was busy with the baby, we had many chances to hone our bareback skills. We could not afford the luxury of saddles. The horses were either so old or so grateful to get a bellyful of feed each night that they obliged us by taking us on rides through woods and valley. Boy, let me tell you, a kid on horseback could really reach those rotten apples!

One Christmas Day, when Bryon was going on two years old, Momma bundled us up and told us to stay *real* busy outside for a good, long time. Meanwhile, she spiffed up the house and laid out her best linens and Grandma's fine old china, chip side down. Her sister Georgia and husband, Mike, along with Cousin Jenny, were going to join us for a Christmas dinner. Mom was trying very hard to make our simple home extra fancy this year, and she was a bit short on time and temper. Dogs and cats were evicted from the house, and Bryon was put down for a nap as Dad tied up the muffler on our aging Chevy for his trip to pick up the relatives. Mike's car was in the repair shop, and the town that they lived in was about an hour and a half's drive in good weather. As we trudged by Dad in our heavy coats, we heard him grumble under his breath. "One more thing for him to look down on, with his pointy little snout and wire-rimmed glasses … nothing is ever good enough around here … city slickers!"

Jimmy glanced at Dad and then at me. "Guess it's gonna be the usual this Christmas, huh?"

"I guess," I replied thoughtfully. "Unless we ride up to County Road 23 and pick up that dead skunk and box it up pretty for Cousin Jenny!" Jimmy grew that silly grin of his, and we raced for the barn to get the horses.

Neither of us cared to ride Dimples, who had tossed us both off several times with impunity. We hurriedly bridled Scott and Sandy and set off for our task, with burlap seed sack and grain shovel to scoop up the poor dead skunk. The horses were feeling just fine as the sun broke out and began to melt what little snow was left on the ground. We headed west into the woods on a shortcut that would take us to the highway and our striped gift. We had been out about a half an hour, when our good, normal Christmas Day changed quickly with an astounding chain of events. Jimmy and I had just crossed a creek, when that seed sack hanging over Jimmy's knees caught tight on a barberry tree branch. Startled, Jimmy pulled his horse up and stopped him dead in his tracks, but I wasn't quick enough to stop and ran right into the back of them with horse and shovel. Well, I don't know exactly where the shovel hit, but I got a pretty keen idea about it, because Jimmy's horse, Sandy, bolted forward and took off through the woods at an angle, with Jimmy hanging on for dear life. I followed the best I could, but the woods were slick with snow and thick with trees and fallen branches.

It didn't take a genius to follow the tracks, and in short order I came upon my brother, who was aground, nursing a bruised rump and just full to the brim with burrs, snaggle branches, and dirty snow. I started laughing out loud, which made Jimmy furious. He came to his feet and snatched at Scotty's bridle. I pulled the horse away, and Jimmy was knocked down. He fell hard and landed in a heap. He wasn't moving. Fear flowed through me as quickly as the laughter had. "Jimmy!" I cried. "Are you all right? Answer me, are you all right?" I didn't dare get off Scotty, especially so far away from home, because he was well over sixteen hands and miserable to make stand still to mount. I called my brother's name over and over, and yet he lay there still and quiet. Worse yet, I couldn't even see his face. If I had, I would have seen that devilish smile breaking a crease along his motionless jaw. "Just stay put, Jimmy! I'll get help! Okay, Jimmy, okay? Oh, please be okay—oh, I'm in trouble now!" With that, I turned for home, and the big sorrel was more than happy to oblige. Moments later, Jimmy stood, brushed himself off, and then set off to find Sandy. He had made a plan.

When I returned home at a dead gallop, Dad had left for his task and Momma was fussing over a big roast in the oven. Bryon was still asleep. I cried and poured out my story, while Momma watched me in astonishment. "Well, I'll have to ride out there—well, I guess—but I haven't ridden in years and I—oh, God bless you two! And Christmas Day, of all times!" she sputtered. She gritted her teeth and said, "Here, now," and handed me her apron. "Watch the baby, turn the roast *down* and the potatoes *up*. Do *not* let those two hounds in, or the cat, and I'll be back as soon as I can." With that, Mom flew out the door in her good dress, with Dad's smelly old barn coat and her barn boots. Scotty was none too happy about being mounted again, and he was slippery with sweat as well, but Momma managed with the help of the fence out front. I didn't dare even look out of the window as she finally made her way out to the road, but at last I peeked, and I saw a vision like a tattered storybook page of Ichabod Crane on his ill-fated journey. I turned and looked throughout the house. It was built, in the fashion of the time, like a boxcar, with rooms running straight into one another. I couldn't help but smile and think of how nicely Momma had fixed it up for us on Christmas.

Bryon woke up in his usual calm manner, screaming for Momma at high C and banging on his crib with his empty bottle, so I went in to get him up. I changed him into his fine new holiday clothing that Momma had laid out and turned him loose, while I put his diaper in the pail on the porch outside. As I did that, our two big dogs beat me to the kitchen door and slid across the newly freshened floor on wet paws clogged with mud. I hollered in dismay, while the cat snuck in, and I was able to grab one mutt by the collar. The other dog disappeared into the living room, where Bryon was opening up our presents at the speed of light under Momma's carefully decorated tree. "Bryon!" I screamed. "You little creep, get out of there RIGHT NOW!" Naturally, he didn't budge, except to give me the old, you-aren't-the-boss look, so I sternly picked him up, legs kicking, and marched him to his bedroom, which was right off the front hallway. Wailing, he plopped onto the floor and had a little temper tantrum, but—oh well—we'd heard *them* before. I went in to find the other dog, but at the sight of all that mud on the kitchen floor, I thought I'd best go in and get the mop before Momma got home.

In the meantime, Momma was having the ride of her life on the brown gelding, whose gaits were rangy and uncomfortable at any given speed. Expecting the worst, she gamely grabbed mane and held on tight through the woods until she came to the scene of the accident. With grim expression and narrowing eyes, she studied the ground before her and what was left of Jimmy. Jimmy had masterpieced a grave-style mound of snow, dead leaves, and forest floor. At the far end, a crude cross made of shovel and stick lashed with jacket string gave Jimmy's work a morbid finish. Momma didn't hear the gasp or see Jim's two huge eyes staring in frozen shock just above the coarse bark of a nearby fallen tree. She didn't hear the tethered Sandy nicker softly to Scotty as she plow-reined him around and headed back for home in anger and relief. Jimmy ran to Sandy and murmured, "Oh boy, girl, we're really in deep *this* time!"

Back home, I peered at the floor, which was nearly spotless again. Bryon, in the meantime, had let himself out the front door. He was feeling mighty fine in his new Christmas clothes and reindeer socks as he headed to his favorite spot on the farm—the goat pen. The sun was strong, and unseasonably warm winds blew from the south as he merrily opened the gate and let the goats out. The ones that didn't come out on their own had his help—he chased them into the barnyard, where our collie dog joined in the folly.

Inside, I turned up the flame on the potatoes atop the stove. I had just opened the oven and pulled out the roast to check it when I noticed a chill wind coming from the living room. I quickly ran toward Bryon's room and saw the front door ajar. "BR-Y-OOOON!" Grabbing a pair of shoes, I dashed out into the cold, mindless of the front door that stood wide open.

The refreshing December air flowed through the house, and the hound named Wilbur was tantalized by the scent of something deliciously rich and warm. He snuck carefully from beneath the gaily lit Christmas tree, which he found to be a favorite hidey-hole when things got a bit hairy, and he walked warily through the dining room to investigate this wonderful aroma. The huge roast, in all of its glory, lay just before him on the rack of the stove. Sensing that it was too hot to touch, he decided to just sit and wait for a moment or two, but his ears picked up at the sound of the noisy, bubbling thing going gangbusters on the front burner. His vigil would not take long. The cat kept an interested watch from her languid position on the kitchen counter, savoring a crock of butter left out to soften.

Momma was nearly home when I finally chased most of the goats down, which took some time, as they were wilder than the dickens and just as scared. The only one I couldn't find was Tootsie, an orphan we had raised in the kitchen—the kitchen! I scooped Bryon up on the run and flew into the house, kicking off my filthy shoes and clumsily balancing my brother on my side so that his slop-soaked clothing would not further wreck Momma's clean, beautifully decorated house. I skidded to a halt at the heart-stopping sight of Tootsie, who had climbed from dining room chair to dining room table and with a wide, playful stance was sampling the centerpiece of store-bought stems and greens. I ran up just as she began her nose dive from the tabletop, effortlessly pushing cloth and dinnerware into a heap, which stopped bare inches from the edge of the table. "Oh no!" I groaned as I caught the acrid scent of burning potatoes. When I entered the kitchen and saw the roast missing from the rack of the stove, I simply let Bryon slide into a pile onto the floor. "Wilbur …," I whispered and promptly began to cry hysterically. Naturally, this got Bryon upset, and when Momma walked in, her anger was temporarily muted when she saw the two of us howling and bawling like a pair of newborn calves stuck in a fence.

"What happened?" she exclaimed. Then, nose turned up like a German shepherd, she said, "What's burning? Where's my roast!" Then, "Sarah, what happened to Bryon!—he's black as pitch!" The final shriek occurred when she whirled about to see her dinner table looking like a shipwreck, with glassware scattered all over and brown goat-hoof prints upon the fancy doily cloths and chair covers. I covered my eyes in kid-fashion and peeked out just enough to catch the sight of Momma spinning around like a top, not knowing which way to go. Actually, she looked pretty funny to me, in Dad's milking coat, with her nice dress splayed out around her knees, but, before I could reflect on that, there was a bit of movement past the dining room that caught my eye. Wilbur! Under the tree—*eating*!

I jumped to my feet, grabbed the broom, and headed for the dog with all of my young fury. Wilbur, perceptive animal that he was, dropped the roast, turned a three-sixty beneath the ornamented boughs, and took off for the front door, scattering loose paper and what was left of the packages in his wake. In horror, we watched as his rear legs caught a strand of lights and the beautiful tree came down with a thump. I remember that the pretty little angel on top managed to keep her footing and landed sideways in the wreck. Her hands were clutched in perpetual prayer, which I thought was an excellent idea at the moment—for myself. Before I could start my Hail Marys, Jimmy walked in with a sack. "Jeepers!" he exclaimed. He exhaled in sheer relief; he intuitively knew that this would surely take the heat off *his* prank. You bet it would!

Things were happening at the speed of light that Christmas Day and, sure enough, as Momma sank into a chair, we all turned to hear the dismal old Chevy arrive in the driveway. Bryon squealed with delight as they walked in. Dad, Uncle Mike, Aunt Georgia, and Jenny stared in silence at the house and at us, until Bryon ran and gave Aunt Georgia a big hug at the knees. She shrunk back in horror at his wet, muddy clothing and face. Dad sunk his hands deep into his pockets, and his expression said, *What's going on here?* Silence prevailed, however, until Uncle Mike cleared his throat, straightened his tie, and peered at the mess with utter dissatisfaction on his pursed lips. Cousin Jenny bobbed impatiently in her sparkling new riding clothes. "Well, I don't really care!" she snapped. "I'm going out riding, and Mom promised me I could ride Dimples!" With that, she bobbed right out of the house and headed for the barn. Jimmy and I exchanged discreet glances.

"What is the meaning of this, Caroline?" Aunt Georgia demanded of my mother. "It is Christmas Day! We traveled a long way to be here, and don't you think you could at least have been prepared? Just look at this place! And what, in the name of our good Lord, Jesus, is that awful odor? We *simply* don't think this is funny at all. "

Momma stood up, drilled her eyes into her sisters', and then said with a dignified smile, "As a matter of fact, Georgia, I went for a little horseback ride today. And decided to open my presents early and redecorate the tree. *And* rearrange the dinner table. Now, I believe, I shall take a bubble bath—you wouldn't mind, would you?" Momma tittered and then she turned to Dad and added, "Oh, Jess, by the way, I burned the beef roast. Please go out and butcher us one of those goats for dinner, would you? Maybe Jeremiah, just for the occasion!"

With that, Aunt Georgia gasped, and the house was filled with an uproar as everyone began to move and speak at once. Dad played helplessly with his car keys, Momma giggled childishly as Georgia stormed about, and then Uncle Mike walked briskly to the door with his overcoat in hand, clearly wishing he was on another planet. Dad offered his car, if they wanted to go home. Jimmy ran up the stairs but returned in time to see Aunt Georgia screaming out the back door. "Jenny! Jenny, darling, come in. We are *leaving right now—Jenny!*"

A moment later, Jenny came hobbling up the rickety stairs in tears. Her hair was a plaster of mud, and her fancy pants had a very distinct heart-shaped blob of brown manure covering her derriere. She was wailing and flapping her arms in a terrific display of humiliation as she was ushered out by Aunt Georgia. "D-D-Dimples threw me!" she sobbed. Dad handed Mike the car keys. He tried to mention that the gas gauge was broken, but he was interrupted—before he could say another word, Jimmy bounced down the stairs and threw a hastily wrapped package into Jenny's arms. "Gee, Jenny! I'm so sorry that you fell—here's your present! Merry Christmas!"

Aunt Georgia snarled, and we all came down to wave them good-bye as they left in an oily cloud of exhaust. "I didn't get the chance to tell you," Dad said in his slow, farmer's drawl, "there ain't much gas left." Momma looked at Dad, and Dad grinned at Momma, and then we all started laughing madly—until I remembered my terrible guilt and hung my head in shame. Momma was laughing out of control, reaching for her apron to wipe the tears from her eyes.

"I'm so sorry, Momma," I started, and Jimmy quickly added, "Me, too, Momma—we didn't mean to spoil your day, especially on Christmas!"

"Spoil my day? Why, that mean, self-righteous old sister of mine and her scarecrow of a husband make me a plain nervous wreck. Heavens, child, you didn't spoil my day—you MADE it!"

With that, Jimmy and I gave one another a grateful squeeze, Dad hugged Momma and Bryon, and then we all went back into the house—kids, cats, dogs, and all—to celebrate what turned out to be Momma's very best Christmas ever.

A Song From Within

Into Wendy's quiet world come a horse and a dream ...

I t was a warm spring day when they met, the girl and the horse, and the air was soft and full of fresh green scents carried upon the beckoning breeze of early summer. In the spacious ring behind the stable, the little gray livery horse pranced proudly, beneath the young girl's gentle hands, defying his years. Although Wendy was deaf and unable to hear the sounds that filled the arena, her soul was singing, and her spirits rode high above the ground as she perched atop Snowball.

In Wendy's silent world, Snowball became her expression and her joy, an avenue of exploration and understanding. For the horse, it was remembrance, perhaps, of days gone by. There had been younger days of energetic desire to please a kind someone he'd known and loved but who was no longer there. As the days lengthened, a love grew between the girl and the horse, bound closely with ties of trust and affection. Wendy spent her many free hours working with the horses for free, and she soon became a familiar figure to those who worked and rode at the barn. Thought she was too small to do most of the heavy work, the owners Bob and Bev would have her groom the livery horses and clean tack. They were always happily surprised at her enthusiasm and outward enjoyment of tasks large and small.

Every so often, Wendy would roam the aisles of box stalls reserved by name for the horses who belonged to private owners. Inquisitive muzzles poked out of the doors as she passed. "Aristocrats with pink pedigrees!" she often told herself as she read the engraved nameplates of the fine horses within the stalls. As she walked by her favorites, they'd nicker a greeting, and as she watched, she strained to feel the vibrations and absorb the sound. As always, Wendy would end her tour with a visit to Snowball, whom she loved the most. No morning went by without a vigorous brushing, and no saddle mark remained at the end of the day.

As the autumn colors painted the trees, business at the small livery stable slowed down, and when the wintry wisps of snow rode the north wind southward, it was obvious that things wouldn't be picking up until the following spring. In December, five of the school horses were earmarked for sale. With a reluctant heart, Bob thought of his younger and more durable horses, and then he consigned the elderly gray gelding. The sale was scheduled for the second week in December, and as the sale date approached, Wendy worked desperately to banish the thoughts and bury the pain in her stomach that would accompany the sale of her beloved Snowball. On the last night, she stayed close to him, enveloped in his frosty breath and warm, furry body. As she bade him good-bye, hot tears fell upon her numb cheeks. She felt so awfully alone now, fading into quiet.

The stall was empty. Stray bits of hay lay uneaten in the manger, and long strands of silky white hair hung captured here and there along the wall. Elsewhere hung the season's happy greetings: Christmas decorations were displayed in the office, a well-decorated evergreen towered in brightly lit elegance, and carrot-laden stockings were tied temptingly beyond reach of the blanketed horses in their stalls. On Christmas Eve, the barn became host to the singing patrons and the falling evening became a festive occasion for sharing the great joy of good horses, fine friends, and warmest of wishes. As the folks began to leave, they seemed drawn back to their horses to give them a final pat and treat, and to secure them for the night.

Wendy stood alone in the tie-stall barn, surrounded by her equine friends, yet bathed in emptiness. As she turned to go, Bob stood ready at the door to lock up behind her. The lights had been turned down, and everyone had gone home to celebrate the holiday with family and friends. Bob handed Wendy a card, which she took, and he motioned for her to open it. It was a beautiful Christmas card, and Bob turned it over to show Wendy what was on the back. It was an offer for Wendy to work at the stable on a regular, part-time basis, with free board in exchange for wages. While her puzzled brown eyes questioned him, Bob led Wendy to one of the big box stalls, and beneath his newly engraved name, snuggled deep in straw, lay her beloved Snowball. The horse gave them a sleepy glance before stretching out for the night. Her heart bursting with happiness, Wendy looked up with silent thanks to Bob, who felt tears come to his eyes. She mouthed a thank-you and reached out to hug the man, who stared over her head to one lucky old horse. Bob smiled, for it was a very good Silent Night, indeed.

Another Log on the Fire

Grab a cup of hot chocolate, and snuggle into that warm comforter. Find out what happens to Huey the horse in this delightful Christmas tale!

It was a saying that belonged to my wife, actually. Whenever our lives were blessed with a happy occurrence, she would say, "Another log on the fire, Charles! Isn't it wonderful!" And so it was—like the glowing warmth of a carefully managed fire, our lives were blessed with the embers of warm family ties and the flames of passion-- and, of course, doused periodically with discouragement and disappointment. I think back to a Christmas not so long ago, precious in memory, and a lesson learned in love.

I've often wondered how I could have been so lucky in life as to have found a wonderful girl to marry and then be blessed with a beautiful child. This predisposed me to a way of life that was bound by the soft shackles of affection and a heart that melted like chocolate on a hot stove. I suppose that to really explain this thing, I should start at the beginning—before Baby Huey, that is, and before our move to this mellow little farmhouse in the rich hills of Pennsylvania.

I am a college professor, born and bred in the dignified city of Philadelphia. Within the cement and brick exteriors of the elderly buildings lay the chords of my youth, which spawned a passion for music and those things

27

that embrace the culture of the city and its people. Not that I didn't enjoy any rural splendors, mind you. My wife, Laura, and I took wonderful trips into the countryside on fresh, breezy mornings. We sat knee high in daisies along tree-lined roads, to breathe in the flavorful air and marvel at the green earth around us. We talked of the day when we would be able to afford a summer home high in the hills, where we could spend time simply soaking in the therapeutic atmosphere of no phones, no bills, no bustle, and no noisy traffic on sooty city streets. One day, while on one of our outings, Laura told me the good news that we would soon be joined by another—she was going to have a baby! We embraced one another, and I felt my spirits soar. A baby! "Another log, Laura?" I teased, and I grasped her hands in mine.

In the months ahead, it became apparent that Laura, although a most cooperative and loving host, was not having an easy time carrying the child. I could only try to comfort her in her difficult moments, not really understanding the gravity nor the extent of the problems she was experiencing. When at last the baby was born, Laura was a fragile shadow of the healthy woman she had been. The child, although born prematurely, was a spunky and normal little girl, whom we named Amanda. The next year was a very strenuous time for us. Amanda, purely our heart's delight, required quite a lot of time and attention—much more than Laura's precarious health could stand at times. Many a night, I would finish my evening's assignments and then stay up well into the morning hours with the baby. With all of my years of teaching, I was truly not prepared for the demands of an infant, nor could I rely on any textbook for the answers. My tender salary was becoming stretched with medical bills, and my disposition was becoming stretched as well. I spent my weekends in the house, catching up on the examination of college-level papers, and we hardly had the time to think about, let along miss, our routine outings to the country. It was also apparent that Laura's health was not improving, and she developed a disturbing lung condition. The doctor's word was that we should move—move far from the city and into cleaner air, where Laura would be more comfortable and in time might recuperate fully. But *move away*! The enormity of those two words sent shock waves upon me. I began to take long walks in the park, while I prepared for the purchase of a home away from Philadelphia—away from my city, my roots, and the source of my existence. I would soon have to commute to my inner sanctum.

On a blustery day late in March, we took a last look at Philadelphia. The cityscape seemed as grim and bleak as my mood as we motored on to our new home. "I still have my job here," I told myself, "And I'll be back nearly every day. It will be fine." If I was at all downhearted about our move, Laura took a different attitude completely. She was excited about the challenges outside our urban past and, indeed, looked upon our new home with a glow in her eyes that had been hidden for a long time. It cheered me, then, to know that things were going to be better—and they were. Laura's health improved slowly over the next few years, and we found our country life to be rich in friendship and in flavor. I developed a keen interest in gardening and spent many a summer evening and weekend morning stooped over the rows of plantings and seedlings, which grew more bountiful with each passing year. I tended the garden faithfully, and it gave me a generous harvest and the firm satisfaction of burying my fingers in the black soil. I toiled not for need but for the appreciation I found for the simple, mindless tasks in life

I also found myself having more time to play the piano, which I enjoyed to the fullest. I hoped one day to hear the melodious notes flowing from the nimble fingers of Amanda but, as much as I tried, I simply couldn't get her to become interested in learning to play. She much preferred running freely about the farm, an outdoor girl at heart.

Amanda was growing into a young girl who found treasures in the meadows and paths and in creatures large and small. Many times she would return from her outings with a small orphaned animal, or from the feed store with a kitten or puppy, only to be told gently that we could not keep it on account of her mother's condition. With moist eyes, she would sadly return her prize—but only after hours spent in the barn with her small fingers entangled in the soft fur of her almost-had friend.

It hardly seemed possible that the years had so quickly passed, but we woke up one morning to Amanda's twelfth birthday. We treated her to a special breakfast, after which we had promised to take her to the county fair. Amanda hurriedly opened the small stack of gifts on the table, and she had barely finished, when we heard a loud knock on the front door. It appeared that her liveliest present of all had come, in the form of my mother, who arrived in a taxi-bus, with luggage and bags and boxes of all shapes and sizes; she surprised us with her announcement that she had come to visit for "a while." Surprise hardly describes it, though, and as Laura's eyes opened wide in what I perceived as shock, I shakily led Amanda's grandma to an easy chair and then took one for myself. As I stuttered a greeting, she crisply informed me that she had written a letter months ago informing us of her intentions. She then clasped her hands on her knees and smiled. "Oh, I'll not be trouble," she said brightly. "You'll hardly know I'm here!" Amanda hugged her heartily and was delighted to show her to our piano room. "Here, Grandma," she said, 'Here's where you can stay!" It wasn't long until the piano had been moved into the living room and wedged ungracefully beside its arch-enemy, the television set. Grandma Humphrey was home. We kindly made the room, but, to this day, I'd like to know what happened to that letter!

The day after her arrival, we all set off for the delayed visit to the county fair. Little did we realize what that day meant or that another new arrival was imminent. Amanda was having a great time at the fair, spending much of her time in the show barns, where she was admiring the fancy, well-groomed animals that came from all parts of the county and whose beaming owners stood chatting amongst themselves. All of a sudden, it occurred to us that Amanda had disappeared, and we began to search for her in earnest. A short time later, she found us. She was accompanied by a most unkempt lad, whose sagging overhauls and pathetic expression drew us immediately to the pair. "Whatever is wrong?" queried Laura, crouching low to peer into the children's faces.

"This is Jimmy," Amanda explained. "Daddy, we've got to save his little horse. He's going to go far away, and Jimmy can't keep him, and his dad is selling him to this man—that man there." Her speech was coming faster, and she was nearly in tears. "Oh, Daddy, it's just a poor little horse, and he needs a home—and Jimmy says this man is not nice---and—and—can't we just take him home? Please? Only fifty dollars, Daddy; could we just take Baby Huey home?" I looked to where she was pointing. I could see a fellow dickering with another, and next to them stood a very sad little creature, indeed. The gelding's ribs poked out from beneath his lackluster coat, and he peered out wearily from beneath a messy forelock.

"Baby Huey?" I queried. "Honey, you know we can't have any animals; we've been through this thing before. I know you want to help your little friend out, but I'm afraid it's out of the question. If it weren't for your mother's health ..." I said, using the usual line.

"But, Daddy," she pleaded, "What if it's okay with Mother? If she says it's okay, can I have him? I'll take good care of him, and I'll—I'll—I'll learn to play the piano—I promise I will!" I looked with uplifted brows at Laura, whose eyes held a touch of mischief in them.

"Sounds like a good deal to me," she said, with a sly look my way. Before I could object, my mother spoke up.

"For heaven's sake, Charles, get going!" With that, she whacked me smartly on the backside with her hard-tipped cane, and before I knew it, I was being hauled and prodded over to the man with the horse, while peeling bills from my wallet. I was soon stammering directions to our house, and Jimmy's father said, "I'll be getting 'im over by 'e is a short," as he stashed the dough in his pocket and led Huey away.

Amanda was beside herself with joy, and the county fair and all of its dazzle was forgotten. I believe she rode the air currents above the car all the way home. She giggled and she wiggled and hugged us all and then herself in happiness. I didn't say much, but the realization was sinking in. A horse? We'd never had so much as a goldfish up until now, so this was going to take some thought. We arrived home, and shortly thereafter, a noisy pickup truck pulled into the yard with Baby Huey aboard, tied to a rusty cattle rack. The man led him to the edge of the truck, the horse teetered on the edge a moment, and then he leaped to the ground with a snort. "Here y'be, young'un," he muttered to Amanda. "He's two year on and could use some grass and a pot o' water. M'boy here raised 'im, and it's hard for 'im to let 'im go, but the cows come first." With that, father and son drove off, but the stricken face of the youngster could be seen pressed against the window of the truck until it passed from sight.

As I look back now, I believe the horse was a turning point in our lives. At first, the animal was just a pet for Amanda, and we were quite glad to see the radiant happiness that it brought her. She was Huey's constant companion. One day, I took a stroll out to the stall where he was kept and was greatly surprised at his growth. Baby Huey had blossomed from a scrawny young horse into a tall, leggy thing who towered over Amanda.

Baby Huey continued to grow … and grow … and before long he was a giant of a horse, fine and proud, with an enormous appetite and zest for life. If I had had any doubts earlier, the love affair ended for me the day when, after shaving, I walked out of the bathroom and into the kitchen to find Huey eating Grandma's oatmeal cookies right off the tray. He was smack-dab in the doorway and looking quite at home. I stood transfixed as the huge horse lipped up the last crumbs, casually backed off, and meandered away. I was still standing there like a dumbstruck turkey when my wife walked by, gave me a peck on the cheek, and started to make a pot of coffee. I stammered and spouted, pointing my finger at the door and then the cookie sheet on the kitchen counter—in complete disbelief at what I'd witnessed. "Oh," Laura said, "Amanda must have left the door ajar. Would you get it, dear?" she asked. "And by the way," she said, "you really shouldn't eat so many sweets this time of day—hard on the digestion."

On another occasion, I awoke to a loving kiss from none other than a stray dog that had wandered onto our farmstead. It marked the end of Laura's bout with allergies—and the beginning of our coexistence with furry creatures. Soon the house became home to the shaggy little terrier and two homeless kittens and, glad as I was that Laura was finally well, I cringed at the change in our home. Now every holiday included treats for the animals, and at Christmas Baby Huey owned the largest and most extravagant stocking on the fireplace, complete with Grandma's homemade carrot patties and apples reserved from the fall harvest.

I began to notice strange things about Baby Huey, whose zeal for pranks at times left me gritting my teeth. One day, I ventured outside and could see him tossing something about in the paddock; first he would flip it high in the air, and then he'd spin it around and around. I moved in for a closer view and saw that he had my good Sunday jacket firmly clenched in his teeth, and other articles of clothing lay crumpled about and beneath his feet. He had managed to pull the clothing off the revolving clothesline next to his pen and was having the time of his life playing dress-up—all by himself. I hollered at him in dismay—and then promptly tore the rear end out of my pants as I clambered over the fence to retrieve the stolen goods. As I approached him, he bounded off, tail high and mouth full of linen. When I apprehended the bandit, I completed my search for the Fruit of the Loom and returned it to its rightful, second-time-around place in the laundry room. I straightened the now-crooked clothesline and, with my shorts flapping in the breeze, headed for the house to change.

Huey became adept at escaping his boundaries, and more than once I had to coax him back from his romps and pound nails in the fencing while Amanda was away at school. We learned of a product called a "hotwire fence," and, after we waited impatiently for a week, the device was delivered in the mail. I studied the box full of insulators and the electrical unit. It was with extreme pleasure that I arranged wire from post to sagging post, while Amanda stood near, beside herself in fearful anticipation of the pain it might cause her beloved horse with the first touch. With black thoughts, I plugged the contraption in and heard a reassuring buzz—it was working and waiting for its first victim. We watched silently as Baby Huey approached us on the other side of the fence, searching for a treat. He walked up with casual interest, but as the long, sensitive whiskers on his muzzle grazed the wire, he snorted and fell back, distrust emanating from his every pore. *Ha! Contained at last!* I thought with a wicked grin. Amanda turned away, and Huey stampeded to the far corner to plot his new strategy, while I rubbed my hands in joyful satisfaction.

I suppose it was only justice that brought us to one gorgeous Saturday evening in the latter days of July. We had invited our minister, the Reverend Roberts, to dinner. Over the past year or so, he had nurtured an affectionate interest in Grandma, who, in return, sported new clothing and a dash of perfume whenever Sunday morning came around. We were all dressed a bit nicer than usual for dinner that evening, on behalf of our esteemed guest, and I decided that I should walk out and take in some air before dinner. What I found was Huey in my garden, sampling the roots and tender leaves of the plants that I had so patiently set in soil and tended. I picked up my shovel from the back porch and took off after him, trying hard not to survey the damage that had been done. As I raced by the squash, I tripped on a row, danced like a scarecrow through the cabbage, and fell headlong into the fence. With tail aloft, Huey hightailed it to parts unknown as I caught myself on the fence, hands wrapped firmly around the only thing I could grab to right myself—the hot wire. With an awful shriek, I fell backward into the rutabaga, from where I could hear my wife's stern admonishments from the back door: "Lands' sakes alive, Charles, not now! Can't you extract yourself from that garden for one evening?" Spittle formed at the corners of my mouth just as the deacon arrived, and as I peered out from beneath the tomatoes, I gave one last look back to Huey, who must have been laughing his horse-guts out. "Amanda, get that horse put away!" I hollered.

"Tell me, dear," I said to Amanda during dinner. "What does it mean when a horse puts his tail way up high?"

"Oh, Daddy!" she replied. "It usually means he's having a lot of fun!" I promptly choked on a mouthful of food and had to excuse myself from the table, prompting a stern look from Mother.

I began to regard Huey with suspicion. Whereas Amanda could do anything with him, he played with me as a cat would a mouse; the horse knew he had my number, and my number came up time and again. Of course, not knowing very much about the equine species, I gave the horse much more credit that I suppose I should have. That talk about dumb animals must have meant cattle, or hogs, or maybe sheep—anything but horses. I was hoping that when my daughter turned sixteen her interests would turn more toward two-legged creatures, and I was right and wrong. Her romantic inclinations included boys, naturally, but they were always accompanied on their visits by horses of their own.

When, for one reason or another, Amanda was unable to take care of Huey, it was up to me to perform the daily chores of feeding him and making his life comfortable, while he made mine miserable. More than once I found myself frozen at the sensation of Huey's soft breath at my neck, and more than once I lost my balance in the mud while he pushed and grabbed great chunks of hay from my clenched arms. The final straw came one day when I rounded the corner to see my mother planted unsteadily upon Huey, hands full of reins and ready for her first lesson. "Mother!" I shouted, "You get down from there right this minute!"

"Oh, pooh, Charles," she retorted, "Can't I have any fun around here? I can *ride*, you know. " With that, she let Amanda escort her around the yard.

"I do remember," I thought testily. It had been on a broken-down cart horse that used to pull a sleigh for us on occasion, when we vacationed in Maine. Her big experience was sitting on its back while it poked along a quiet logging road.

I began to think in terms of a horseless life and spent nights awake plotting to rid myself of the beast. He was the bane of my existence, that four-legged demon, and I blamed him for more than one gray hair now beginning to sprout across the top of my dome. I kept my thoughts to myself, naturally, until the opportunity arose one day in early August. Amanda had graduated high school, and her plans had turned to college and the years ahead. I sat her down on the front porch one evening to have a heart-to-heart talk about the days to come and the many challenges that faced her. She had chosen a good college, out of state, and would be gone many months of the year. I felt that this was my chance to rid us of Huey once and for all—not that I expressed this delusional idea to Amanda, who sat stonewalled at the idea of losing her childhood companion. "Sweetheart," I began tentatively. "You'll be needing a car, room and board, and books—lots of books, and lots of other things. We simply cannot afford to keep a horse while you're away. And ... I've been considering a move back to the city. We may sell our home here. " Amanda stared off into the meadow past the road, and her eyes became liquid. The old, familiar softening was encompassing my midsection, and I was just about to reconsider my words, when she said softly, "I know, Dad. I know I have to make the choice, but ..." She sat in silence, and I glanced over to where Huey was munching grass, oblivious to our conversation. Amanda stood up and, with a voice that belied its emotion, told me to do what was necessary.

Amanda hadn't been gone a week when I put into effect the hours of planning it took to get rid of Huey. The ad was in the paper, and after sitting by the phone a few nights, I realized that horses weren't exactly a hot seller that time of year. I received only three calls, two parties of which showed up to see the horse. The first party was a father who brought out his thirteen-year-old boy. The boy seemed to know everything about horses, but, in fact, learned something about the depth of the ditch alongside the road where he fell off. "Well, he's probably just a little frisky," I said hopefully. "My little girl rides him all over!" With a last rub of the boy's rump, son and father departed quickly. I unsaddled Huey, who calmly bit my shoulder as I struggled to remove the saddle. The next couple who came out undoubtedly knew less than I about horses, and as we sat discussing our mutual ignorance, we were treated to a most obnoxious show of horse behavior from Huey, who was tied close by. He chewed at the rope, he pawed the ground until it shook, and then he reared up several times against his restraint. The two took off in a hurry as I called desperately after them, "Can't we talk price?" Once again I ruefully disrobed the horse, who stood as quiet as a lamb once they drove away.

After many more inquiries, I finally found a prospective owner in the agricultural division of the college at which I taught. It appeared that they needed donated animals for feed research. After reassuring me that Huey was going to be fed and not going to become part of the feed, they picked him up to live happily ever after within the confines of the rural schoolgrounds. I was elated! Here was a home that even Amanda would approve of, and I was much relieved to wake up each morning without the realization that the very first being I would confront would be a hungry horse. No more trips to the barn on freezing nights; no more heavy buckets nor lugs to the loft—no more Huey! My lovely days lasted for three or four weeks, until one Saturday morning. As the sunlight gleamed on the frost, who should appear but Huey, neighing his delight at finding himself in familiar surroundings, held in hand by a sandy-haired young man next to a trailer. "But what happened?" I stammered as I fumbled with the tie of my robe at the door. "You took him because you needed him?" The young man held the excited Huey, while he explained. "It seems your horse, here, sir, is quite adept at unlatching his stall and untying his lead. No trouble, actually—we've been able to handle that, you see, but yesterday it caused quite a ruckus in the lab. That is, *he* caused quite a commotion, sir." The student looked down at the ground and tried hard to maintain a serious expression. "In fact, if it hadn't been for the boa, the dean might not have been so upset."

"Boa?" I asked weakly.

He continued, "We were able to catch the monkeys easily enough, and the mice and the guinea pigs and so on, but the boa is still missing, and, well, sir, it's been quite a scene back there."

"Mice? Monkeys? What are you talking about! Speak up, young man!" He went on to explain that Huey had been unloosed under somewhat mysterious conditions in the lab building, and with his penchant for strolling through doorways, he had meandered into the small-animal lab, upsetting cages and aquariums in his quest for the small alfalfa pellets which were fed to the various creatures there.

"Wasn't his fault, sir—senior pranks, you know." And with that, the boy handed me the lead shank and returned to his truck and trailer. "He's quite a horse, you know," he said as he backed out of the driveway, grinning from ear to ear.

There I stood, shivering, on the icy driveway, hair in clumps, holding Huey. He was delighted to be home and had a most indignant expression on his face at this humiliating experience. "Wasn't my fault," he seemed to say, "Hear that, old man?" and then he pulled me toward the barn. I did my best to follow, dragging along the stones in my slippers and trying to slow him down. Sounds of pain emitted from my throat as into the barn we went. At the barn, he stepped on my left foot while charging into his stall. Because it was awfully hard for me to close the stall door while I was howling and holding my toes, he took advantage of the opportunity to bound past me for a triumphant run outdoors, his tail as high as a flag on a pole.

Something had to be done! Amanda was due home in a few short weeks for Christmas break, and she believed the horse to be gone. I'd be doggoned if I was going to sit by and watch the happy reunion. It was now or never. I took a trip into town in the wee hours of the next morning to make a few more inquiries. At the small country café in town, I came upon a group of local farmers. I learned from one husky fellow that a man came through town once every two weeks and bought old, crippled, or otherwise undesirable animals from the cattle and dairy people. "Fact is," the man said, "he was just here not two days ago, but I can't be sure if he'll be back before Christmas. And I can't say as he'd be willing to pay you much, either, but he'd take him and perhaps find him a good home." I left my telephone number with him and his cronies, who were sipping hot brew at the counter. I went on my way, feeling pretty poorly about the deal but, nonetheless, determined to have the matter settled at last.

The following week flew by, and my guilty conscience grew with every frost-filled morning that I tended to Huey; he was so cheerful and bear-like in his warm winter coat. Amanda was due home in just a few days—perhaps reluctant to come home without the familiar whistle from the paddock to greet her arrival. Time was getting short! I received a call only one day before her expected arrival. Huey was to be aboard a truck to downstate New York in an hour, if I was still interested. The truck arrived and, after many reassurances from the driver that Huey would be treated well and sold to a good home, I watched as he was loaded onto the truck. He clambered up easily, as he had when he'd been a real baby so many years ago. As the vehicle lumbered away, I heard his final whinny, and my feelings reeled in a mixture of relief and remorse. I stood there quietly in the snowy lane as my memory took me back to green mornings when before me would trot my lovely daughter on her horse, so married in motion, so devoted in their betrothal. I thought of Christmas mornings when Amanda would race out to the barn, just in pajamas and coat, and with her long hair blowing in the wind, she would show Huey her most precious new possessions and treat him to a piece of strawberry toast. When finally my numbed hands begged to go indoors, I walked heavily past the brightly decorated tree and sat down with a sigh, still in my coat and hat, feeling much a victim of my own crime. The fireplace was cold and empty, and above it hung the colorful stockings that adorned it year after year, with the exception of one—the largest one—the one that belonged to Huey.

Amanda arrived home early, quite unexpectedly, just hours later. After a joyous welcome, we sat about the living room, which sprung alive with chatter and a lustrous orange glow from the roaring fire at the hearth. As the fire subsided to embers and our talk turned to silence, Laura cleared glassware, Grandma arose to announce that she was retiring to her bedroom, and my eyes met Amanda's somewhere between the mantle and the floor. Amanda gave me a halfhearted smile, and I knew she was trying hard not to think about the stall in the barn, empty save for a bed of straw and uneaten strands of hay. Instead, she picked up a cat and stroked its thick fur. "Amanda," I began gingerly, "I know you've been very busy at school, and we've missed you something terrible. We haven't had time to discuss it, but …" My words floated off miserably as she looked on.

"It's all right, Dad," she replied softly. "I know how very hard it must have been for you." While I was pondering carefully my choice of words, we heard an exclamation of "My heavenly days!" from Laura, who ran from the kitchen window to the front door and threw it wide open. In a mixture of amazement and astonishment, we sat frozen to our seats as Baby Huey blew the welcome whinny and let himself in. Crystals of snow decorated his steaming flanks, and as Amanda flew over to him to give him a great, slushy hug, I found a better position for myself in the bay window, safely behind the piano.

Huey was home! How he had escaped that truck was anyone's guess—and of no real importance. Amanda looked over to me, with tears streaming down her cheeks and with an expression of joy I'm sure I'll never witness again. "Thank you, Daddy—oh, thank you! Thank you for changing your mind and for keeping him! It's just the most wonderful gift you could ever have given me, ever-—ever—ever!"

Being a modest hero, under the circumstances, I just managed to croak a weak "you're welcome" from my perch. I added more forcefully, "And that's the end of the subject!"

Laura looked over to me with a knowing smile and said, "Well? What are you waiting for, Charles? Put another log on the fire!" I picked a giant of a log, big enough to burn all night, and as I stoked the embers, I looked at my family in what I knew was going to be our home forever. I raised the poker to them in a mock toast and couldn't resist. "A very merry Christmas," I said. "And, Huey, this one's for you!"

For Donna

There's always one Christmas you'll remember forever …

*L*ooking back, there was one Christmas that I remember as sharply as what I am feeling now, with pitchfork in hand as a shivery north wind hits my face on this sun-drenched day in December.

I was just a boy at the time, growing up on the outskirts of the city of Chicago. We lived in a rambling brownstone on an orderly street lined with lots of big old houses. The little front yards were edged with sidewalks to skate upon. My friends and I chased imaginary outlaws down cobbled alleyways and through backyards framed by small, painted fences and towering staircase porches. In the wintertime, we were never too far away from a warm kitchen or corner stove. For me, the trials of a harsh midwestern winter meant more snowballs, more ice-skating, and more fun. Christmas in the city bestowed a stately display of gleaming strings of lights hugging the evergreens in homes and businesses, and twinkling beads of brightness fringed gutters and windowpanes all along the avenues and high atop the roofs. It was a kid's fantasy, and we spent many hours thinking about that new bike sitting behind the frosted pane at the Marshall Fields Store just a half a block away from the subway station.

I was a boy of eleven, and it was just a few days before Christmas. Out of school, and after a morning romping in the splendor of outdoor fun, I carried my ice-encrusted jacket and soggy mittens to set atop the radiator in the kitchen. I heard my mother on the telephone, saying, "Why, Walt!

We'd be delighted to have you here for Christmas! Yes, please, do come!" When my Dad arrived home from work that evening, Mom related her conversation with Uncle Walter. Mom told him, "He says that they can stay a day or two on their way to Indiana to see Mitzi's mother. It would be so good to have the family together for the holidays—it's been so long! He also said he was bringing Donna and that she was a little hoarse, but it shouldn't be a problem. The connection was so bad, we finally hung up, but they'll be here sometime tomorrow evening. I can't wait! But, who's Donna?" she asked as she bent over the stove.

Dad replied that he wasn't too sure, but maybe she was a cousin. "Hope she's not bringing the croup," he muttered, and then he looked away, thinking of his childhood and his brother, Walt.

Walt lived on the farm left to him and Dad by Grandpa, and we didn't often get a chance to visit them . Dad had grown up on the farm, but after his days in the service he had found a relentless desire to explore and conquer the challenges of the city. I often envied my cousins, who flourished under the huge Iowa sky, who rode horse-back to gather the cows, and who took skinny-dips under swaying willow tree branches. Why, they even drove the truck across the bumpy fields and could drive the old tractor. The smoke from his pipe spiraled slowly upward as Dad sat in his chair that day, lost in his memories. Mom did the dishes, and my brother and sister and I hustled off to plot our plans for the crowded, wondrous days ahead.

The day before Christmas Eve crept into early evening, and our excitement was hard to contain. The kids perched alongside the front windows, waiting for Uncle Walt's arrival. With each approaching set of car headlamps, we'd bet on whether it was theirs, only to watch the receding tail-lamps in disappointment. Finally, a large old panel truck rumbled its way slowly along the snow-packed street to our house, and as Dad ran out to move his car, the door of the truck swung open and out spilled Aunt Mitzi and five kids. Dad grasped Walt by the shoulders in a massive hug, and we all got reacquainted in the doorway, between blasts of frigid air. We all settled into our living room, now buzzing with chatter and laughter and news. Dad disappeared with his brother, and the next thing I knew we were greeted by a huge, grizzled dog, whose tail swept the air with every stride. "Couldn't leave Jinx and Bobo behind," laughed my cousin Paul, and as I looked on in glee, I saw the tail of a striped tomcat disappear beneath our large sofa. He was plainly unhappy with his holiday home.

Mom and Dad and Uncle Walt and Aunt Mitzi were in the kitchen when I ran in for some soda, and things didn't seem just right, it seemed to me. Dad looked a little strange, and as I looked on, I heard him say, "How in Sam Hill are we going to keep *her* here? This isn't Clarksville, you know!"

"Oh, quit fussing," Uncle Walt answered. "It's only for a day or so, and I'm to take her to a new home in Indiana---don't worry so much!"

Mom just giggled, once the initial shock wore off. "Good heavens, Peter! That's Donna! Donna's not a little *hoarse*—Donna's a little *horse*!" And, with that, she fell into a spasm of uncontrollable laughter. Mom was always a good sport, and I guess the party wine had hit home. I left them like that—Dad clutching the bottle of bourbon, Uncle Walt plucking a stray potato chip from his overalls, and Mom and Aunt Mitzi laughing hysterically. I couldn't wait to give the good news to my brother and sister! We all ran out, jacketless, to see Donna.

Donna was indeed a little horse, pure white, with the prettiest brown eyes I'd ever seen and a coat you could bury your fist in. Walt had surreptitiously unloaded her in the alley and parked her in the garage, where she quizzically explored her strange stall amidst the tools and rakes and paraphernalia adorning the brick walls. Walt had prepared a bed for her and secured her to the wall, explaining to us what makes horses happy. Dad showed up and busied himself with covering the frosted windowpanes with cardboard Santas while nervously peeking out to see the tenants on either side of us. "You know, Walt, I don't think this is allowed here," he began, but Uncle Walt just kept on breaking up straw.

"Horsefeathers! If that old beater of yours doesn't mind, I don't suppose Donna will, either! As long as she doesn't do any talking, who's to know the difference?" Walt said, and he winked at me. "And who do you think built this city?" he added. "Horses—and manpower—you bet!"

I don't think any of us slept too well that night, with the exception of Bobo. The dog snored so loudly I thought he'd peel the paint off the walls, but

Christmas Eve dawned just as pretty as you please, and I awoke straight up in bed, grinning ear to ear. Donna! It was still half-dark and awfully cold out, but I snuck out to greet her, leaping through the crunchy snow to the door behind which she stood. I slipped inside the garage door and was rooted to the spot, awed by her presence. She nickered and shook her head, which I took as a motion for me to come over. As my fingers caressed her silky mane and cool gray muzzle, I felt something stir within my eleven-year-old frame that told me this was the closest thing to a miracle that I might ever experience. I guess I must have been there for some time, before the door burst open, and all the other kids bustled in with outreached hands and energetic chatter. Before I knew it, Donna was no longer mine alone. How we fussed over that little horse! We spent the whole morning going to and from the garage, until lunchtime, when Mom took Aunt Mitzi and the girls downtown for the afternoon to see the Christmas decorations. Dad and Uncle Walt did a bit of sightseeing on their own, much of which I suspect was done from a cheerful perspective atop barstools with Dad's buddies. My brother took my cousin Paul on an elevated train ride, which left me alone with Donna. I sat there in the bright straw before her, and my imagination took me on glorious rides over dusty lanes, races above grassy hilltops, and walks along ragged creek bottoms. Closing my eyes, I held her wisps of mane in my hand and guided her as we danced in fields of yellow and then lay peacefully beneath shady oak trees.

It wasn't long before a loud knock at the door made me jump wildly to my feet, scaring the horse and sending the water bucket flying. I cracked open the door to find my good pal Tracy standing there, shivering in the cold and begging to come in. As I opened up, he came inside and stood in wide-eyed amazement at the sight of the horse in our garage. "Is she yours?" he asked incredulously, and in a childish way I wanted to say she was, if only for that moment. I told him why she was there, and he asked if I had ridden her.

"Yeah," I lied, "lots of times, on the farm."

"Geez, how about showing me?" he asked in unabashed admiration, but then I began to feel really dumb.

"No, can't take her out—someone might see," I replied. Tracy looked at me for a long while, and then he dared me. When I refused, he double-dared me. I bit my lip and thought of my daydreams in which Donna and I soared over those green fields, and then I thought of how much I wanted to take the dare. He put up a stake of marbles, and we shook on it. "Tonight, at two," I said with steely eyes and watched him shoot me a sidelong look.

"Got it," he spat and then was gone.

Knowing what lay ahead didn't make it easy for me that evening, even during the meal of roast beef, something we didn't have too often in those days. The feeling of trepidation grew throughout the Christmas Eve festivities, which lasted well into the night. As everyone said their last goodnights and turned in, my heart was fluttering and my mind fled from the thoughts my conscience was working hard to interject. I lay in bed with my eyes wide and watched the glow of the streetlamps as the time approached for me to go. At long last, I tiptoed past Bobo, whose deafening snores covered any bumbling I might have produced. I was dressed and almost out the back door when I stepped on something and heard a piercing shriek. It scared the dickens out of me, until I saw the cat skidding around the corner on his toenails, heading, no doubt, for the safety of the sofa once and for all.

It was snowing softly, and I stood there in the darkness, gathering up the courage to trek to the garage where Donna and Tracy awaited me. "Ride that horse, sure," I mumbled to myself. "All I ever rode on was an old milk cow, and she grazed the whole time—I must be nuts." With that, I walked on, hoping that Tracy had forgotten or gone to sleep. When I stepped into the garage, I knew I was wrong. Tracy was waiting there expectantly, so I went up to Donna, untied her, and walked her outside to the alley beyond. She lifted her head with interest and began to sidestep and paw the ankle-deep snow. I drew a deep breath and prepared to clamber onto her back with the help of a nearby garbage can. With only her halter to guide her, I was suddenly on her back, and the blood beneath her skin made my britches feel all nice and warm, as the radiator did after a day of sledding. Donna stepped off down the alleyway in a jolting walk; she examined each shadowy corner and snow-hooded garbage can with interest. We went about six doors down, and since I didn't know how to turn her around, I pulled back on the rope, and was most relieved to have her bend her head and turn on her own. Feeling quite a bit more like John Wayne now, I let go of my death grip on her mane and walked proudly the stretch of twenty yards or so back to my house. I was getting ready to slide off, when the dog next door burst out barking and howling at the apparition he saw in Donna. I fell straight down into a snowbank, which pretty well took care of those warm britches. As Tracy high-tailed it over, I lost my grip on the lead rope. The last we saw of Donna, she was rounding the turn at the end of the alleyway. At that moment, I believe I was introduced to true terror.

"What if we can't find her? Golly, Trace, what if she gets lost—oh, me and my big mouth!"

When we got to where we thought she'd run to, Donna was nowhere to be seen. The glow of the amber streetlight cast a serene softness as we continued to trot along the sidewalk, following her tracks so clearly defined in the new blanket of snow. With each car that passed, we'd duck into a doorway, hoarse and blowing with exertion. All I could think of was Uncle Walt going out to the garage Christmas morning to find her gone. Guilt flowed through me like water, until we slid around a final corner and saw Donna. She stood there in the midst of the community nativity scene, picking through the straw and looking quite at home next to the lifelike mule and cow. It seemed to be a good time to start praying, so that's what I did as I caught her up and led her home. We managed to sneak home down the alleyways without too much trouble, and all that remained as evidence of our hijinks was the vanishing hoofprints and a few astounded late-night partygoers who thought they saw something they couldn't have seen. Tracy, sworn to secrecy after I bargained back his marbles and most of mine, disappeared and legged it home. After a certain last prayer, I slipped back into bed and allowed sleep to ebb the last quivering thought from my tired mind.

As I sat in church the next morning, a hymn rang out in a beautiful chorus, and my thoughts were dreamlike as I relived the events of the night before. At home, we spent the day playing with our new toys and sharing in the joyful spirit of a wonderful day enhanced by the warmth of giving and the gladness of being together. The day passed in a blur; soon it was late, and Aunt Mitzi was packing the last of their belongings in preparation for the next leg of their trip.

They left the next morning, and as we stood on the front porch waving them off, I heard a muffled whinny from within the confines of the trailer. I wished with all my might that I might someday see Donna again, but that day never came.

On this Christmas morning, I feel again the wonder, the fascination, and the fear of that special night as I watch my son trotting through the deep drifts astride the snowy white gelding that I bought him on this, his eleventh, Christmas. His face is glowing in the fresh, frosty air, and I feel his heart race—as mine did, so many years ago, atop Donna.

We still visit the city, but the farm life suits us just fine. Something about that little Donna lit a fire within me that only a sweet country breeze could put out.

A Long Time From Home

Get closer to the fire, and warm up to a wilderness story—and a small Christmas miracle.

It was a magnificent Christmas morning. Crit sat on his horse atop the knoll and took in the decorations, one by one, as the morning sun made him tip his hat to shade his eyes from the sparkling, shimmering carpet of snow. Like fine crystal, the delicate ice particles clung to the pine needles, and the pine cones shone from their frozen castles as cardinals and blue jays splashed color from one bough to the next. The creamy blues and grays of the lowland blended with the brilliant sky to create a palette an artist would hunger for. The vestige of the moon faded, and yet the man lingered, thinking back to a day years ago when he had been moved, on this very special day of his very ordinary year.

He had been riding that morning, too, nearly five years ago, if the marks on the rough-hewn wall meant anything. That day, Crit had been returning from a month-long trip on his gelding, Hawk; Sister, the pack horse, had been heavily laden with the fruits of his expedition to the high country, where the trapping was good. The wilderness, although bountiful in its natural resources, was an unforgiving host to those who ventured through its crevices and forested floor. A man had to be very careful up there alone, so Crit, as always, was silently grateful for the safety of his animals and himself as he made his way carefully through the loosely packed pass of stone and precarious rock. Crit had been a trapper since the time he'd been abandoned as a young boy of fourteen; it was the only thing he knew. As he rode along, he thought back to those early days, the tough ones, to a young boy who had hauled a skid of skins on his back down these same treacherous mountain stairs. He never saw his dad again, after he'd been left to fend for himself in confusion and adolescent pride. He did not care.

There was no family to go home to, yet his need was great to return to civilization and the outpost where he would cash in his rough-skinned wares. It wasn't for anyone special, just human company and coffee brewed on a stove instead of over a lonely fire.

As the day darkened and marbled the sky in the gray-black hue of a winter evening, he felt a presence behind him. He pulled the horses up and glanced back, but, with senses honed by animal-like instinct, he decided it was not that of a grizzly. Just the rattling fall of a vagrant rock glancing off a distant ledge disturbed the chill air. *Just the fall of a rock,* Crit thought—not enough to make a man draw his rifle or seek safe ground. Crit continued on for a while and then bedded down for the night about half a day's ride from the outpost. He stripped Sister of her bulky, frozen load and tended the horses carefully as the flames flickered hesitantly in his early campfire. He bent to straighten his bedroll, and again the sense of something close made him stiffen and listen. The horses, tired and quiet, would be sure to give him sign of impending danger from bear or timber wolf, but they stood without apprehension and appeared relaxed. Crit laid his gun close by and went about his dinner of wild game, the variety of which most townsfolk wouldn't think to feed their dogs. He turned in for the night, sleeping the deer-like sleep of the hunted.

Daybreak came and with it a hoarish cast to the valley below; it would be a warm, misty day to make the snow heavy with perspiration and the travel slick. Crit had no trouble dousing the embers in the dampness. He meticulously packed the mare again, and then cast his leg over the back of his horse and, with lead rope in hand, began his journey downward. He reached the bottom of the pass and gave his horses a needed drink in a creek, which was beginning to swell widely with the melting snow. It had not completely frozen over, and clumps of ice swam with vigor as the banks grew to accommodate the new water. It was there that he spotted the horse, who appeared to be a dark buckskin, with a big, white blaze extending on down past his nostrils. It was hard to tell about the rest of him, as he was shrouded by the darkened limbs of the winter tree line. "So you're the bandit," said Crit out loud with some relief. He whistled at the horse out of curiosity, but the horse never moved. Even at the distance, his ragged coat and thin body were evident. Crit picked his horse's head up, and he urged him back up the path to where the other horse stood. The buckskin watched and then turned from sight. The path narrowed down to a single footpath ahead, so Crit turned Hawk back to the creek and, beyond that, to the trading post with its warm handshake and welcome respite from the cold and solitude of the wild. *Ah, what the hell*, he thought. *Some old stray looking for a meal.* Tired and chilled, he went on his way.

"It's a good start," Crit declared after his pack was unloaded and thawed a bit to reveal a good many prime skins of beaver, muskrat, and mink. It was good, too, he thought, to talk to the men there and good to be within walls of log and mud and rough-milled lumber. He wasn't thinking much about the horse, until a shrill whinny cut the air outside, coming through the thin, waxed pane at the window. No one gave it a thought, but Crit's mind riveted back to the shadowy horse who had followed him down the mountain. Not worth mentioning, he thought wryly. Or worrying about. The oil lamps were dimmed, and it was time to turn in for the night on a borrowed bed with fresh gingham linens and feather pillows. Tomorrow he would head out for his journey home, packing with him the money, food, and sundries to carry him through until his next trip.

The morning dawned with angry skies and the threat of a storm. Not a pleasant day, but not one to hold Crit back from his solitary trek to his somber little cabin a day's ride away. There were plenty of places to seek shelter along the way, and more than one nor'wester had passed with no more than a brief snow shower. He tipped the innkeeper generously and nodded good-bye.

"And a Merry Christmas to you as well!" shouted the fellow, and Crit waved in response. He shook his head. Christmas! He wasn't even too sure which day it fell upon. Whether it was today, tomorrow, or yesterday, he did not know. He had never had much of a Christmas to celebrate, and he had decided long ago he never would. In a few hours, he arrived back at the same creek crossing, which had swelled and ran with vigor over the rusty-colored rocks and shale. He went in knee-deep to water his horses before heading back to the flatland, where he found himself gazing to where the buckskin had stood the day before. Only the sway of raw limbs in the blustery wind gave presence to the spot, and with only detached interest, Crit mused on the fate of the horse.

Hawk picked up his head then, and with water dripping from his muzzle, he fixed his ears on a point downstream. He nickered and continued to stare diligently at the riverbed just beyond view. Crit gigged him, and they walked down the riverbed to find the buckskin gelding lying on his side in the water, his body partially submerged, his head barely clearing the rocky ledge of the bank. His tail was a club of burrs and tangled branches and his coat a dull mass covering little more than a half-fed carcass. Crit grimaced as he saw the barbed wire twisted cruelly around the horse's neck and imbedded deep in his throat, which was raw where the horse had tried to rub off its miserable captor. His throatlatch had swelled; the horse was severely debilitated from lack of food and water, and now his wind was being cut off by the relentless wire. His eyes were closed. "Dead or alive, Buck?" Crit asked, and in response, the horse's nostrils flickered and an eye opened to reveal an expression so full of pain and suffering that the man drew his gun from its scabbard. He took a close bead on the horse's head but, as he steadied his horse, the buckskin sensed the end and, with strength born only of years of flight and fear, made a game attempt to get up. He succeeded only in falling back to the frigid water, and with a long, low groan, he gave up his life to the man and the cold, swirling stream.

Crit lowered his rifle, dismounted, and swore as the icy water grabbed his pants legs. He cautiously approached the animal and ran his hand along his neck to the barbs and the blood-caked mane. With a sigh and a shake of his head, Crit drew a halter, and with little objection from the horse, managed to get it on the horse's head. He tied Sister up to a stout little tree and mounted his sturdy gelding,

Hawk, after running his lariat through the buckskin's halter.

Keeping a dally, he mounted and urged Hawk on up the bank and to the small pine-framed clearing just yards away. The gelding tried to get up with the tug of the rope, and his legs flailed about on the slippery rock. He fell back, and once again Crit shouted and spurred Hawk on. Again the buckskin was moved to flight, and this time he managed to get his legs under him enough to half-fall, half-scramble up the bank and onto dry ground. He wobbled there momentarily as Crit quickly stripped off the dally and ran to the edge of the river, flapping his hat and swinging the end of the rope. The gelding took three more steps and collapsed. The wind was now beginning to whip down the cut, and the branches all along the edges of the creek were swaying madly as Crit sized up the situation. "Damn," he said beneath his breath. His feet felt as if they were frozen, and the poor buckskin horse surely would not live through the impending storm, let alone the night.

The snow began to fall, and the wind mocked the silence of the woods as it groaned through the pass and made the treetops whistle and wave in a delirious frenzy. Crit quickly unsaddled and unpacked his horses and tucked them deeper into a shelter of thick, impassive trees. He returned to the downed horse and with cold, stiff fingers cut the wire from his neck and lifted his head to remove the rest of it. The buckskin offered no resistance, even as Crit pushed and tugged on him to better position his bulky pack items alongside the horse to help warm and protect him from the wind. He covered him with saddle blankets and canvas and then went about digging up the driest branches and downed wood he could find for a fire. He banked his fire with river rock to keep it from the greedy clutches of the wind and snow, and soon he had a flicker going, which he coaxed to flames. The storm lashed out from the west and from behind them, and the fire had a chance. Crit parked himself in close proximity to the horse, whose faint breathing was barely noticeable in the wind and swirling snow. His makeshift wrap was certainly inadequate for the situation, but it would have to do. Crit snuggled down for what promised to be a very long and desolate night, during which he'd have to get up several times to refurbish his fire and face the dampness and cold. He thought of his warm cabin and soon fell into a fitful sleep, wherein a ghoulish horse with wild, abandoned eyes had him trapped beneath the water and ice in a raging river … his legs were pinned, his arms stretching helplessly for safety. His head went under—

With a start he awoke and shook the snow from his hat brim in order to look at the gelding. He saw the prone, still body, the spare frame so listless and spent, and he saw a beaten animal whose only hope of survival lay with the man whose hazel eyes studied him in the reddish cast of the fire. Crit thought back to a dog he'd had as a boy, and suddenly he felt the rush of buried emotion that he'd felt when the dog had died in his arms long ago. He could feel the dog's rough, thick coat and see the deep brown eyes that had regarded him with trust as his life ebbed away. The dog had had guts, and he had had courage, and he was the only thing that the grizzled trapper could remember loving. It was unassuming love, fiercely protected, and the crushing loss now filled Crit with a desire to save the horse. He lay back down and closed his eyes, restless with his thoughts and memories.

The snow had stopped its mad descent when Crit arose shortly before dawn, and the sky above was clearing save for a few high, wispy clouds that streamed past the moon, now stark and ice-bright in the blue-black sky. Crit fed the fire to a roaring blaze, and the heat from the rocks now radiated warmth. He pulled out some beef jerky and sat chewing slowly while watching the buckskin horse for any signs of improvement. A day and three meals later, Crit kept his vigil in the dark. The burrs had been picked from the horse's mane and tail, and Crit had cleaned and disinfected his neck. The fire shadows flickered and fell on the inert form as Crit studied the evening sky. He picked out the brightest star and decided it was the Star of Bethlehem, beneath which another vigil had taken place and ended in a miracle. He wished for another one, a smaller one. As he dwelled upon that thought, the horse beside him heaved his neck and head up to an upright position, and the startled man jumped back, spilling his coffee clear down his chin and all over his heavy woolen coat. Crit wanted to shout with relief, but he knew better and just watched as the horse began to weakly search the ground at his nose for wisps of forgotten summer forage. Crit slowly got up and gathered a bucket of meal for the horse, who nibbled faintly at it, head bobbing with effort. "You son of a gun," Crit murmured. "I think you just might have a shot at it." He watched the horse eat until long after midnight, when he finally retired to his bedroll. "You son of a gun."

The next day, Crit backtracked to the outpost, loaded horse feed in Sister's packs, and then returned to his makeshift camp with the supplies, settling in to his routine of stoking the fire, hunting dinner, and waiting.

It was another day gone before the buckskin attempted to rise. When he did, his legs were weak and his loins drawn, and like a newborn colt, his efforts were aimed at staying on all fours. Crit kept up his offerings of water and grain, and the horse accepted the man's hand with neither fear nor suspicion. What Crit had initially thought to be scars beneath the matted coat was a brand on the horse's near hip. Crit's fingers read the mark of a top outfit that spanned thousands of acres in the adjoining territory. He touched with wonder the spots of white hairs that grew in along the horse's withers on either side. "You were a usin' horse, you were. I think you're a long way from home, boy," he said softly, "and a long time from there, too."

In a matter of a week, the gelding grew strong enough to move about and drink from the stream. His neck was beginning to close up nicely, and the soreness was eased by the remedies Crit used to draw the infection. The horse began to move about and forage on his own. One morning, Crit slung his saddle on Hawk and loaded Sister. He walked up to the buckskin, placed his gloved hands on either side of the woolly head, and said, "It's time to go, fella. You're welcome to come, and I'd be glad to have you, but it's your decision." The horse looked at him, and in those eyes Crit could see intelligence and breeding, pride, and something else—like the defiant stare of the bull elk or the wise, calculating gaze of the cougar; it was there. The man turned to go. "Either way, I know you'll be all right."

He mounted and rode off for home, down through the bed of rocks and running water. The buckskin followed them to the edge of the woods and stopped, ears flicking back and forth in obvious consternation. Crit turned once to look and then continued on. When he finally couldn't take it any longer, he stopped Hawk and turned in the saddle to peer back. There was no sign of the gelding. He quickened his pace, feeling sheepish about his disappointment, and went on. Soon he neared the cutoff for his home trail. Once he thought he heard the parting of underbrush behind him, but it was only a large muley buck skirting the horses. He reached his small homestead, turned his horses in the pen, and fed them before storing his gear and supplies. "I sure do wish you luck," he said to the open meadow before him as his eyes played over the tree line in the distance. Finally he turned and went indoors, closed the door behind him, and started up the old woodstove. It felt good to be home, and as he busied himself, he tried to put the memory of the horse out of his head. He never really succeeded.

Yes, it was *a special Christmas*, he thought to himself nearly five years later as he sat on the hill overlooking the splendor of that grand Christmas Day. He thought back to the campfire and to the storm, to the bright star in the sky, and to the small miracle that had occurred beneath the snow-laden branches of those western pines. He thought again of the horse: his bony, shivering frame, his reluctance, his surrender and then ultimate acceptance of the man. Crit also remembered the stifling disappointment he had felt when the sunlit horizon offered no sighting of the horse. He remembered, too, the day when he had gone to fetch the wood at dusk, and his eyes had caught the faintest movement way past the trail marker to his house. He felt as he had felt that day, when the blur became the form, and the form became the horse.

"You bet it was special," he said aloud from his perch in the saddle, and his hand reached up to finger the scars on his horse's neck—way up on his neck where the barbed wire had cut him and nearly taken his life. "You made a good decision, boy." With that, man and horse descended the hill to the valley below, a pair of old orphans who'd found in one another a small Christmas miracle.

The Homecoming

It was the phone call I remember best. I was lying in my bed, like some frozen chunk of snow, as I held my breath and tried to listen to the conversation oozing through the crack in my bedroom door from the hallway beyond. Mama was crying, and Dad was trying his best to soothe her, and I couldn't bear to listen anymore, so I put my pillow over my ear in order to muffle their voices. My thoughts pounded sharply through my head. Johnnie was coming home. He was coming home for Christmas.

The next day dawned late: a dim, dreary prelude to all of the black, wintry mornings to come. I dressed and pulled on my overalls to do the morning feeding of our six horses, who waited expectantly for my arrival. The jingle of Corky's nameplate against his dog collar alerted them, and they nickered their welcome in the cold, blustery air as I opened the barn door and threw on the lights. "Hey, guys—and girls!—good morning. At least I *think* it's a good morning." My attentive audience followed my every familiar move in hungry anticipation of their morning grub. "Guess what?" I said out loud in the barn. "Johnnie's coming home." I went along and fed each horse but, before the last flake of hay was thrown, I found myself stilled—as if the dark and the dawn's red glow were beckoning me to stand quietly and listen to the rhythmic munching of the horses chewing their grain. Tears formed then, those hot ones that come quickly and burn but never fall. I hurried through the rest of my chores and, upon returning to my room,

I dressed for school, putting aside my fear and my hopes until the time came.

The time came quickly, for it was the third of December, and in only one week my brother would be home for Christmas. Johnnie was twenty-one and five years older than I was. He was my only brother, and in our younger days I had looked up to him as if he were a statue, or some God put upon the earth for me to admire and emulate. He was kind, and he was strong, and he rode our horses like I'd never seen horses get rode before. "Just a natural!" Dad would boast, and Mom even quit her nervous fidgeting while she watched John stroke along with his mount in some odyssey of motion that brought him and the horse to an almost magical transgression of oneness that was stunning to behold. Trophies lined the wall, from conquests near and far, and the prospects for bringing home a world championship were not far off.

My mom was always afraid for us. Maybe she feared the horses themselves but feared more the dangers of the sport for the rider. "Too many Reader's Digest articles, hon," Dad would say as he winked and tacked up yet another young horse for Johnnie to work in the arena that he had built just outside the barn. I always envied my brother for the glow that he put on my Dad's face and for the pride he seemed to exude without any of the motions or braggadocio. I'd take his hot horse and walk the animal out, wishing all the while that it was I who had put the sweat on his back and the knowledge in his head. I simply lacked a little something when it came to working with the horses, but I kept on trying and hoped it would come with time.

Well, it did, after a fashion, and by necessity, as it turned out. One day, when Johnnie and I were in the barn goofing around, he was feeling awfully cocky, for he said to me, "Brett! Go get that sorrel filly out—she's going to get lesson number one!" I took a halter with me and walked cautiously into her stall, for the mare was new to our barn, just three years of age, and a wild, snorty thing. The filly wheeled around once in her stall as I stood quietly waiting for her, but instead of moving closer to me, she spun again and nailed me in the knee with a wicked kick that brought me to the stall floor in agony. I called out for Johnnie immediately. "Johnnie! Get in here; oh, please, get in here!" He came flying down the aisle, lifted me from the floor, and set me down on a bale of hay nearby. Then he closed up the door on the filly, who stood stalky-legged and belligerent, feeling confident at her victory over the haltering session. "You all right?" Johnnie asked with concern, and I grimaced my okay with a weak nod of the head. Johnnie turned to the horse.

"Let's go," is all he said as I sat there struggling to right myself while holding my throbbing knee. He managed to halter the filly and he led her past me in long, determined strides to the arena beyond. The filly followed skittishly behind, but she stood hard and fast as he saddled her and then led her out to the middle of the arena. I watched with mean satisfaction as he lunged her hard and long, harder than I'd ever seen Johnnie work one before. She was blowing hard when he bridled her, and then he lunged her some more, until the sweat darkened her coat and her nostrils flared like dinner plates. "How're you doing?" he shouted over to me, and I shouted back, "Just fine!" I massaged my knee, knowing full well how Mama would feel if I limped ungracefully into that house. Johnnie discarded the lunge line and warily stepped up into the saddle, gathering up the reins on the snaffle bridle. He proceeded to untrack the filly by pulling her head to the right.

For a time there, I could not remember what happened next, but after about a week or so it came back to me in a blinding flash that practically brought me down to my knees again. The little mare had ridden right off but, as Johnnie had turned her this way and that at a walk, she had caught her breath, and her outlaw nature had kindled into a half-buck, half-trip that triggered Johnnie to pull her up and kick her over. With that, the sorrel mare's eyes had just kind of turned white all around, and she had lunged to the right, pulling hard on the bit. She had tried to escape the pressure, and in doing so, she had put herself off balance. She'd reared up high and then down over backward, and I'd watched my brother disappear beneath her broad brown back. Then, as quickly as it had happened, there was just the dust and the silence—and his still form lying in the dirt.

At first, the doctors had thought it might have been a coma brought on by head injury, but, upon further examination, it had appeared that there was nerve damage in Johnnie's back, the extent of which was unknown, as it was being aggravated by the swelling of the surrounding tissue. Mom had been devastated and Dad pale and shaken, but I never once thought that Johnnie wouldn't come out if it intact—he'd just wake up one day with that great smile and the "give me five!" and we'd go on like always. I'd waited for him, and I knew he'd been waiting, too, but that day never came. Johnnie came out of his coma to enter a world of blurred vision and slurred speech, of physical handicap and mental barriers that stripped us of the young man who had once flourished in his love of life and its challenges.

Very slowly, he recovered his speech and manual dexterity, but it was clear that he would not walk again. We had him home for a while, but the hope and encouragement we gave him only seemed to hurt him more. Johnnie was depressed, angry, and abusive. Then the silence set in like a sullen January sky. Finally Johnnie demanded to be released from our care at home, perhaps from our eyes, and he was placed in a rehabilitation center where his needs could be met without family ties. It stung us all, and for me it was like losing an arm or a leg, or perhaps more like losing my future. Two years went by without change. I got better at riding, mostly because Dad wanted me to, but my heart wasn't in it, and his sad face never held the beaming approval I'd witnessed when Johnnie was training the horses. We just kept on, though, and although Dad's visits to the barn were less frequent, he insisted that I keep up the schooling and the showing in what I thought was some crazy idea of his that Johnnie would be back to take over again one day. Johnnie had the magic, and the magic was gone from our little farm like a dove out of a hat.

It was snowing hard the day Johnnie arrived home. In fact, we didn't think he would be able to make the trip, but, when the van arrived, we all dashed out to meet him in the swirling snow and the cold. We wheeled him up the walkway and into the house, where we stamped off our boots, smiled a lot, and made small talk. Mama kissed Johnnie on his wet cheek and clasped her hands together in a nervous, yet happy, way. "I'll make some hot chocolate—would you all like that? Johnnie?"

Johnnie sort of nodded and turned his face to the living room, where the fire was kindled. He then looked up to Dad and me. "Nice to be home," he said softly, and as we acknowledged his quiet greeting, I could tell Dad was close to losing it. I knelt down, grabbed Johnnie's hands in mine, and gave him a big hug, which gave Dad a chance to busy himself with the fire and to collect himself. We had a nice talk over big mugs of steaming hot chocolate, and after a while it was just Johnnie and me, sitting there at the table facing one another after the long, lonely absence.

"I sure missed you," I said to him. "I'm so glad that you're home."

He looked at me and replied, "Take me outside, Brett; I'd really like to go outside."

"You nuts?" I returned, "It's a blizzard out there!"

"Outside," he said again.

We sat in the storm on the porch, Johnnie in his wheelchair and I on the stoop, and we watched the icy crystals sweep and sway as darkness fell upon us. It was a long time, it seemed to me, before the blanket across his knees was white with snow and he asked to go back inside. We came into the house, and I peeled off my clothing that was now soaked with wet snow. I handed him a towel, and he handed me his hat and jacket. I was happy to see that familiar ruddy glow on his face, but I had the feeling that it was only from the cold and not from inside him.

Two weeks went by, and I arrived home from school for Christmas break to find Johnnie sitting in front on the television set, which was his customary place for most of the day. "Hey, brother," I called. "How about a game of chess—it's been a while since I whipped your butt!"

His answer was a shrug and a "No, thanks," as he returned to his show. I dressed to go out and do chores, and I watched him as I put on my coat and boots. I noted for the umpteenth time how the back of his head was becoming part of the living room wall, or so it seemed. He never once spoke of the horses, even though he knew that I spent the time I did with them, and we were all afraid to even mention the word *horse* in the house while he was present. While it was getting more comfortable to be around this stranger whom we loved and knew so well, it was a strain on all of us where the horses were concerned. They were as much a part of our lives as he was, but we honored Mama's wishes and never once mentioned their existence.

It was just before Christmas, and I had a lot of time to spend with my brother. He was restless and moody but never once said what was bothering him. He didn't ask to go back outside again, even at my urging. I was helpless to do anything but try to please him with my company, but as our days together grew long, I felt a taut resistance on Johnnie's part to let me in. I knew it had to do with the accident and his frustration, but I felt hurt that Johnnie wouldn't grant me that which I felt was mine—his love and trust. I kept my feelings under control until two days before Christmas. I'd been out in the barn a while, working a horse who would simply not come around. I'd tried all my tricks, and a few more besides, but the bay gelding just balked, sulked, and resisted me—much as my brother did in the house. I'd gotten mad and whipped the horse, forcing him to do far more than he'd ever been asked to do, and as a result, I'd set his training back by weeks. I'd left the horse standing saddled in the frigid aisle, shaking and trembling, his heaving sides dripping sweat and the steam from his back rising high in the air. "Serves you right, Wonder Boy," I muttered. I knew it was wrong, but I left him like that, and I walked out of the barn and up to the house. Mom and Dad weren't home from work yet, and in anger, I pitched an ice ball at the back-door light. As luck would have it, I hit it dead on, and it shattered.

I swore out loud and then walked into the house, to where Johnnie was sitting with his dark mane pressed against the back of the wheelchair, watching yet another trivial afternoon game show. "Dang it!" I shouted to his back, "What's the matter with you, anyway?" He spun around and faced me with an expression I'd never seen before. It was a mixture of spite and anger and two years worth of hope turned sour—and he was ready to vent. Well, so was I! Flames shot high as we began to shout at one another. With every move I made, he'd spin and turn, and we faced each other like a couple of alley cats: one wounded, one strong. I accused him of not caring about his family, and he countered with our utter lack of understanding of his feelings. Words flew back and forth, until we finally exhausted each other's rebukes and stared at one another in a dead stalemate, which lasted until he deftly whirled himself away from me. I stood there with clenched fists and cruel words ready, but then I broke. I broke, and I felt the pieces falling all about me in shame and in fear of what I had started. I walked into the kitchen, and my mouth opened, but no words came out. I stood there with helpless hands, while Johnnie struggled to open the door and escape what he had feared the most—his lost future, in the form of his young, healthy brother.

I handed him his coat and his cap as he struggled to get the awkward chair through the door and down the ramp to the barn below. He allowed my help as we entered the barn. I dragged the heavy metal wheelchair inside to the dirt floor. With the closing of the barn door, there was only the rustling of the horses and the sweet, clean smell of hay to greet us. *Don't hate me, Johnnie—oh, please don't hate me,* I silently begged of him. He stared at the horse on the cross ties, whose coat was still matted and steamy. "New one," he said without question in his voice.

I replied, "Yeah, new, but not too well broke. Good bred, but not too bright, you know? Dad likes a challenge." I stuck my finger in my throat to emphasize my words. Johnnie thought that was funny, and he started to laugh, and as he did, I did, too, until we were both laughing—well, practically screaming—as we continued to cut up every last short-wired, dimwitted horse we'd ever had around the place. We were still grinning when I stepped in low to hug Johnnie and grabbed him as tightly as I could through his bulky jacket. It was a big, terrible, desperate hug that left us sobbing into one another's arms like two big babies. We were weaving, and crying, and squeezing hard with just his useless legs to keep us from dancing. We finally had made contact after the years of distance—and, by God, it felt good. Awfully good.

What a great Christmas we had that year! It was the best Christmas of all, complete to the most delicious tenderloin Mama had ever cooked and to the house full of people. Every last Christmas toast we'd ever made to one another was repeated over generous doses of laughter, and old stories, and a few pure lies, just for fun. Johnnie had finally come to terms with himself and with his injury. He had never stood taller in my eyes than when he'd announced his special present to Mom and Dad, who followed us out to the barn with some leftover laughs and more than a bit of confusion, glancing at one another in trepidation.

The saddle that we had made up was a jerry-rigged thing, but when I heaved Johnnie into its crude cradle, I'd never felt more confident in him. He picked up the reins and looked out into the arena with that old, familiar glint in his eye. Mama held her breath, and my Dad didn't move a muscle as Johnnie slowly maneuvered the obedient horse in a wide, slow circle and then back to us. I threw up my arms in a "victory" stance, just as proud as proud could be. "Give me five!" I shouted. Dad was all choked up, and Mama was wringing her hands with worry, but as Johnnie put the horse into a slow, graceful spin, I knew that the dove was back. Johnnie was home for Christmas. Johnnie was home for good.

The Chestnut Man

It was Christmas Eve, and we had just come in from doing our barn chores. "Well! It's about that time, don't you think?" Dad said cheerfully, gazing upon his three children sprawled on sofa and floor. Jason, my fifteen-year-old brother, had just inserted a new rental video that we were anxious to see, while Lucas, my six-year-old brother, waited patiently with crossed legs on the floor. With cheeks still red and stinging from the cold, I waited for the inevitable.

"Dad," I started, "don't you think we're older now, and these little family-night games on Christmas Eve are kind of ... well ... silly? Well, not really silly, but ... like, old fashioned?"

Jason perked up with a hopeful look, but it deflated when Dad replied, "Heavens, no! It's fun! It's great for the family, and besides, you know your mother needs tonight to get ready for ... Santa Claus!" I watched him wearily, especially during the dramatic pause and imaginary drumroll before the jolly red giant's name came up.

Lucas nodded enthusiastically. "Yeah," he cried, "she's gotta bake *cookies* and clean the *chimley*!" Jason and I exchanged glances, and he clicked off the VCR. As the older sister, I had made my stand but, once again, had failed to get the horse in the barn.

"So, what's the plan, man?" Jason queried my father. "Not another sleigh ride! Please, Dad—last time the shafts broke, and we had to pull the thing all the way home!"

"While Lucas got to *ride* it home," I added in a whisper, through clenched teeth. "And we don't have to go help old Mrs. Tannenbaum tonight, do we? I mean, like maybe the day after Christmas we could give her a hand," I said, remembering the "good deed Christmas" when we had shoveled out her entire milk cow pen, not knowing the cow wasn't actually living on the second floor, just above the tons of old manure.

"And Lucas sat on a bale of hay," Jason muttered.

"No," Dad said kindly, "she passed away last fall."

"That's too bad," said Jason, hardly containing his mixed emotions regarding the news.

"No," said Dad. "I've got a really interesting evening planned! We're going to see Arthur!" Jason rolled his eyeballs, and I sat slack-jawed on the couch as Lucas jumped up and grabbed Dad's hand.

"Let's go, Daddy! Let's go!" Then he peered quizzically up and asked the question on everyone's minds: "Who's Arthur?"

Arthur, it turns out, was a neighbor to the west of us, who lived in a scary old farmhouse. It was set all alone in a huge grove of trees that shrouded his run-down buildings. Even his ancient apple tree delivered tired, pitted fruit, hardly worth snitching. As we walked up the rutted gravel road, Dad made us all hold hands and sing Christmas carols—which were pitched to new heights as Jason and I played finger wars, trying to make each other cry out in pain. Apparently, Arthur was ready for us, as it appeared that he had locked up his nasty hound and left a dim porch bulb burning. Dad rapped on the door, but no one answered. "Maybe he's asleep," I said hopefully.

"Yeah, Dad, he probably needs his nap—better go," agreed Jason. Finally the door opened with a great groan, and there stood Arthur—all four and a half feet of him! Lucas's eyes grew wide; he'd never seen a grown-up so close to his size.

"'Mon in," said Arthur, and we all trundled through his doorway. "'Ave a seat," he offered. With resignation to Dad's latest Christmas adventure, we sat on Arthur's worn couch and awaited our fate, which I expected to be a very long and boring evening of tall tales and who knew what else. Dad stood and announced that Arthur had a very interesting story to tell us. After we'd all settled in, little old Arthur clasped his hands and began to speak.

He began his tale of the chestnut man and his chestnut-colored horse as Jason and I listened with less-than-rapt attention, mentally ticking off the minutes until we could leave. As he talked, however, his marvelous broqued voice carried to us a remarkable history about the very ground we rode our horses upon each day. It was hard not to become entranced with the story of this chestnut man, who would fill his sacks with chestnuts and have his horse carry them into town, so that everyone might have roasting chestnuts for their holiday festivities. More remarkable, the man did none of this for his own good but, rather, donated the proceeds to the local orphanage, so that the children would have a few books, some new clothes, and a grand Christmas party each year. The chestnut man would walk to collect his treasures, with the help of a long pole. More than one chestnut would find itself firmly planted into the ground along the way, thanks to the special cane. The brown horse followed solemnly, performing his duties to perfection. Over the course of many years, a fine number of trees grew tall and strong. The man gave the grove to the town so that they might forever enjoy a special Christmas blessing bestowed upon them by one old man and his old brown horse.

When Arthur finished, we sat quietly pondering his words and the unselfish acts of the chestnut man. "What happen-enned to him?" asked Lucas, wide-eyed with curiosity.

"Well, the old horse died," said Arthur. "The man buried his faithful companion beneath the biggest chestnut tree in the area. Less than a year later, the chestnut man died, too. I helped bury him next to his horse." Arthur looked down at his hands, and I thought for a minute he was going to let loose a tear. "He was m'friend," he said slowly. "Your great-uncle was my very best friend."

We left the old farmhouse, gripping one another's hands once again and lost in our own thoughts. "That was really neat, Dad," said Jason.

I looked up through the dark branches into the star-studded sky and murmured, "Awesome!"

"Can I have a chess-nut horse one day, Daddy?" Lucas asked.

As we walked on, approaching our warmly lit home, Dad stopped us short. "Look there," he said. We followed his gaze to the biggest tree in our pasture as he let a proud smile lift the corners of his lips. "The tree? *That* tree? You don't mean—I mean, that's not really *the* tree, is it really—Dad—really *the* tree?" I stuttered. We crawled through the fence and walked in silence to the huge, stark tree, and Dad bent down to scrape the snow away from a small, sodless depression, recently cleared of grass and leaves. Dad reached into his pocket and pulled out a penlight. As we gathered close to see, he illuminated a crooked, discolored plaque. It was hard to read the words, so he read them to us.

> We buried him deep
> And his soul was set free,
> By his old chestnut horse
> 'Neath this old chestnut tree.
> This comes from my heart
> And upon bended knee:
> 'Twas a good friend of all
> 'Twas a great friend to me.

"Wow," I said softly. "This was real special, Dad."

Jason nodded his assent, while Lucas huddled over the grave with a solemn look upon his cherub face. "What was grade-uncle's name, Dad?"

"Well, son … it was Lucas John Perry."

Jason and I just looked at each other in the dark. The kid got everything.

The Christmas Passage

Dreams do come true in America ...

Jon sat exhausted, too tired to stand, too little emotion left to do anything but stare down between his legs at the straw on the floor. He was in the little shed where Niss and he had lost the fight to save her foal. It was very quiet now, with just the sound of the wind as it hissed and blew through the tiny cracks of the walls, and graceful flakes of crystalline snow danced elitely under the eaves. The hot perspiration now chilled him through his flannel. The flickering oil lamp burned low and then out, as if to snuff the memory and ease the misery of the two whose loss was too painful to bear in the glow of the flame. Jon stood up, pulled his jacket about him in the doorway, and stared out to the rough-hewn poles planted in the hard ground beyond. Like evening sentries, they stood in line on the stark landscape, glinting with frost. They were to have been the beginning of the new barn—that spacious, warm barn that would have housed the horses and the cattle, the hay, the crops, and the equipment that now lay encrusted in frozen mud just past the shed. Jon turned his collar up as the cold seeped into his very bones. The kind, numbing effect took his thoughts back to the time when the struggle for the land and his hopes for the future had been a fierce force driving him onward. Now, he was not so sure.

It had not been that long ago that Jon and Flora had moved to the homestead of graceful meadows and carpeted woodland. They had been filled with the dream of a home they could build with a lifetime of hard work and determination. They had come to this town in America with untiring energy and soft-spoken manners, and they'd bought a small site high in the hills, where they began to work the land and improve the simple homesite as their time and monies allowed. With them they brought a legacy of their homeland, a trio of young stock from their native Norway, with the hopes of building a small band of full-blooded Fjord ponies. Although the horseflesh in the new country was of fine bone and character, the Fjord ponies were a vital, living link to the thousands of miles separating Jon and Flora from their homeland. When Flora gazed out from her kitchen window and saw them grazing, she thought of the beautiful running rivers and misty highlands of their Norwegian home, and when Jon hitched the team to the heavy plow he felt a strong assurance from their tireless haunches and unfailing dispatch of their duties.

Tough and sure, these gallant creatures were an integral part of the plan. They helped cultivate the fields and bring in the harvest, and they worked the wagons and hauled lumber from the forest. Needing little in the way of feed to keep them strong and muscled, they had hearty constitutions that had kept them sound and disease-free, even during the long and arduous ocean voyage to the new country. Jon was very proud of them, even though they did receive curious glances and mute attention when his occasional journey to town drew them away from the fields. The townsfolk drew silent when they approached, and it was difficult, if not impossible, to evoke conversation from any of the people. Only the storekeeper who filled Jon's orders spoke to him, but he was impatient over Jon's broken English and struggle to relay his needs. It was always uncomfortable for Flora when she accompanied Jon, as the rude stares and muffled comments never failed to invade her sensitive eyes and ears. She felt shy and diminutive, and her silence was interpreted as aloofness by the ladies of the town, who, in turn, ignored her completely. They declined to invite her to the town functions or the women's social affairs. Church itself was not much of a relief, except that while they were in the small, white frame church, Jon and Flora were as much a part of the congregation, in the eyes of God, as anyone else. The smirks were left outside "lest the good Lord frown down upon he who would cast a stone," as the preacher reminded them all. Even Gustaf and Niss, the sturdy team of Fjords, made a strange pair tethered beside the other teams of horses, their honey-and-cream-colored bodies and thick, bristled crests in stark contrast to the deep, earthy-toned coats and long, smooth manes of the other horses.

In August, the minister invited the congregation to a summer picnic. The whole town came out for a day of fun, which included contests to test the strength of man and beast alike. Flora made a batch of delicious pasties for the potluck dinner, and Jon entered his team in the pulling contest. At the end of the day, everyone gathered up their belongings and left. On the way home, safely out of earshot, Flora exploded in a deluge of angry words. "These people are unspeakably crude!" she shouted into the warm, breezy air. "They refuse to treat us with anything but contempt and ridicule, and we have done nothing to warrant their terrible manners. Not a one of them would put their lips to my pasties—as if they were poison! And that Elisa Eldridge—why, her tongue is wagging from the moment she sees us to anyone who will listen. They are just awful!" With that, Flora broke down and cried great tears of frustration.

Jon grinned back and pulled her close to him on the seat of the buckboard. "Perhaps Mr. Eldridge was not too pleased when our little Norwegian ponies outpulled him and his fine team of blacks in the horse pull! Oh, the look on their faces—all of them!" he said triumphantly. Clovis and Elisa Eldridge were the most wealthy and influential people in the town. They gave lavish parties and Eldridge sat on the town board, as had his father before him. Eldridge blew great clouds of cigar smoke about the steps of the church and touted a large billfold; he swaggered about while obviously enjoying his position of privilege. He was also quite blatant about his political views, including his disdain of immigrants. Jon's laughter made Flora quit her tears for a moment as she, too, relished the memory of the moment when the men for once had stopped their raucousness—and stared in dumb amazement as Niss and Gustaf had heaved forward and dug into the earth. Their momentous blast of power had sent the load across the line three feet further than had any of the teams that had gone before.

Flora smiled a little smile of satisfaction, and then her brow furrowed again. "This is no place to raise a little one. They will be the same, if not worse, to our child, and I'll not stand for it!" Jon pulled the team in. He grabbed Flora by the shoulders and asked the question that had awaited them since their marriage. She nodded, and Jon's heart soared to new heights with joy. A child!

"We're going to have a child!" he shouted, and with renewed energy, the team of Niss and Gustaf sprang away from beneath the slap of leather to canter freely down the trail, homeward bound.

A barn up before Christmas and a baby on the way—well, two, actually. Niss was about to bestow upon them the miracle of their first Fjord pony born in America. Their second Christmas in America would certainly be special, and yet so much had to be done before it arrived. As the leaves turned to yellow and then to brown, Jon worked from daybreak to dusk, first with the harvest and then with the task of cutting the tallest of trees into posts for the barn. He worked with backbreaking speed and determination, and even the team of ponies came in from the day's work, long past feeding time, too tired to eat with any gusto. The progress was swift, however. The poles were soon arranged in position, and the lumber was on order to complete the sides. For days, Jon and the ponies toiled to hoist the poles into the tediously dug holes. At last the job was done, and each post was tamped securely in the hard-packed earth. The barn! Jon's dream of the large, beautiful barn was becoming reality, and as the sun set on a clear day in November, his content and pride were nearly too great to contain.

By the next sundown, his troubles were nearly too much to bear. The bank would not lend them the money for the lumber, even with the farmstead for collateral. They would not honor his future crops as payment, either, even though the harvest had been bountiful and the land ripe with promise.

The next few days, Jon and his team were idle. There were no axes to grind, no trees to chop or trim, no poles to pull the merciless miles home. Flora busied herself with household chores and beckoned Jon to help her prepare their winter's store. Jon listlessly went through the motions and spoke nothing of his deep resentment and tight-lipped anger. "There will be next year," Flora said gently one afternoon, and Jon's sudden outburst startled her into dropping a crock.

"Next year!" he cried. "Next year will be the same story! We'll have to save up for years to pay for it in cash. Not to mention where we will house our stock for the winter. We'll have to sell the cows, Flora; I'll not keep them without proper shelter. What money we have left over from selling crops will have to go for our own food and feed for the horses. There will be very little left over!" he fumed. With that, he stormed from the house and stomped off to sulk.

Flora knew only too well that he was right. Oh, why were they so ill-treated? She put her hand to her abdomen and prayed for a miracle. "Just one more, Lord ... just one more."

What began as a very normal day in mid-December turned into a nightmare. Jon had just returned from town with a load of lumber that he had stubbornly purchased with money gained from the sale of two cows. He was unharnessing his team, when his ears picked up the faintest sound in the wind coming from the south. Town was due south, and the wind that day blew clear and strong, carrying with it the barely audible chimes of the church bells in the valley below. They were clanging quickly, almost desperately, it seemed, and Jon and Flora strained to interpret the strange midweek alarm. They looked at one another, and Jon quickly refastened the buckles on the half-harnessed team. Gustaf and Ilka, the mare who had taken the pregnant Niss's place in the traces, were less than enthusiastic as they headed back out on the road with Jon and Flora securely bundled against the cold. Jon and Flora wondered what emergency might lie ahead, but they were prepared to help if they were needed—it was the way of the old country.

When they arrived in the town square, people were gathered, and horses and riders were dashing here and there in haste. "What is happening?" Jon shouted in his broken English.

A small boy answered excitedly, "The train has derailed in Luther Valley and Petey Eldridge is on board! It's upside down on the mountainside, and the telegraph line went down, too!" He dashed off, and although Jon and Flora did not understand all of his rapid-fire talk, they followed a group of wagons and horses rushing out of town on the well-traveled road to Lutherville, where the train was to be met. In about an hour, they arrived to see another group of people animatedly explaining to Clovis Eldridge that the train had indeed gone off the tracks at a point just west of town. The access was difficult on account of the trestle that lay between the mangled machine and the town. Elisa Eldridge sat white-faced and pale on the seat of their fancy carriage, her hands knotted in anguish.

71

Once again, the group of wagons and horsemen took off at a good clip, and soon they came upon the wreckage of the train. In a breathtaking view, one could see that the locomotive lay broadside in the wake of downed pine trees, and the rest of the cars were either on their sides or at sickening angles on the side of the mountain. There were vague sounds of people's cries coming from the train, but the sounds were quickly swallowed by the fickle wind and the chasm that lay between the rescuers and the train. The train trestle stretched long and sinister, linking the two sides of the chasm together in a brace of timbers, bolts, and iron rail.

As Jon looked over the situation with the others, he wondered how they were going to reach the stricken passengers. To make things worse, the sky above menaced with low, ugly clouds, and the winds were picking up to hamper the men who were already edging their way along the treacherous trestle. Their path was slowed with heart-stopping moments as they struggled to keep their balance in the wind. Jon's mind raced to the lumber in the bed of his wagon, and he hurriedly began to cut the cords that held the stack. "Help me!" he shouted to the men who stood watching the drama, but they hesitated. "Help THEM!" he enjoined, and he pointed past the ravine to the train. The men then started to come and load their arms with lumber. Jon grabbed the nails and his hammer and strode to the tracks. With strong blows, he laid the planks down between the rails, one after the other, and they created a walkway across the trestle. He spaced them carefully, far enough apart at the seams, so they would reach the other side, but they still fell short by twenty feet or so.

Already the moans of the injured were evident as the rescuers began trying to bring them out of the wreckage to the tracks above. It was slow work, and it was doubtful that anyone could be carried to safety without stretchers. The planking would help the footing, but there were those who couldn't walk! Already the weary rescuers were beginning to feel the dangerous effects of the cold, and their numbed feet could not be trusted to walk across the howling void. Jon made it back to the worried crowd who were watching, and he shouted, "I'll need that wagon!" His eyes were fixed on a small flatbed wagon with a single horse hitched to it. He commanded, "Unhitch the mare!" and with gestures and signals, his words were obeyed. He freed Gustaf from the doubletree and hitched him to the smaller wagon. He then sized up the track and positioned the pony alongside. "Lift the wheels when I say," he said as best he could in his broken speech, and quickly the wagon was astride the iron rails. The onlookers watched in a mixture of curiosity and apprehension. "Hup!" John cried as he instructed Gustaf to go ahead. The big wooden wheels lurched along the ties just outside of the rails. Slowly Jon led Gustaf forward, quietly urging him on past the edge of the mountain over the abyss below. The trestle seemed to stretch for a mile ahead as the heavy wheels clumped over the ties.

The pony picked his way slowly over the planks, with Jon at his head, trusting his hooves to fall only inches apart at a time. Although he showed no sign of spookiness, the pony's ears flickered back and forth quickly— but his trust in the man at the fore was clear and unerring. Jon and Gustaf picked their way across the trestle as Flora watched in runaway fear. If something were to happen to Jon, she could not bear it, and if something happened to Jon's stallion, their dreams of a band of Fjords were finished. Flora glanced over to see Elisa Eldridge slump over and nearly fall from her seat on her carriage. Flora quickly ran to help. She helped Elisa straighten up, and she sat down next to her, taking her by the hand and holding her close. Wordlessly, they sat and waited.

Jon had nearly made it to the other side, and everyone held their breath when Gustaf took his first steps on the plankless trestle where the boards had run out. The pony hesitated only once, and then he peered down to see each and every tie, slowly placing his hooves on firm wood. It seemed to take forever, but they finally made it to the other side. Prayers were renewed.

When the first cautious load of injured was delivered safely, the pony's coat was gleaming with effort. When the last load safely crossed the threshold, he dripped with sweat, and with trembling legs he was led away. Grateful hands toweled him dry—hands that shook Jon's in sturdy acknowledgement and then patted Gustaf on the back and neck with admiration. The train, once smoking and alive, now lay dead and cold, her passengers safe except for the engineers who had been thrown from the locomotive and could not be saved.

When Jon and Flora returned home several hours later, Niss was deep in labor. The day ended sadly, but Niss was alive and, for that, Jon was grateful.

After the excitement died down a few days after the train wreck, life was pretty much back to normal for most. Soon it was Christmas Eve, and Jon and Flora had finished their traditional Norwegian dinner and had settled down to play a few hands of cribbage near the warm stones of the hearth. Flora shuffled the cards and smiled. "I love you," she said.

"I love you, too," Jon said tenderly as he looked around the simple room. "We have a beautiful home, Flora, and I owe so much to you. I know how much you must miss your family." His gaze traveled past the shutters to the land beyond.

Flora said, "I have you, Jon, and we have our dreams. Our barn will be built, Jon, it really will! Your ponies shall have a grand home, too. We will do it together. Next Christmas shall be even more special. We'll decorate the stalls for Niss's baby—I know she will deliver safely next time—and Ilka's, too, if we are lucky!"

She was so sure, Jon thought. "Next year," he replied, nodding. "A promise." He stared at the Christmas tree adorned with Flora's precious ornaments, many of which she had insisted hold a special berth on the passage to America. Jon kept his doubts to himself all through the night as they fell asleep upon their warm feather bed. "Next year."

They came at the break of dawn. First there was the clatter and clang of the heavy wagons loaded with lumber, then the buckboards of warmly dressed men, whose boisterous voices could be heard for miles around. Laughing and joking, they were ready to flex their muscles for the day at hand. The ladies followed in carriages laden with fresh food and gifts in gay packages. Children jumped from the wagons as they rolled to a stop, and the older ones ran to hold the horses and move the supplies. A small group approached the house and stood there hesitantly in front of the doorway, where Jon and Flora appeared in their nightshirts, mouths agape and clearly confused.

Clovis spoke first. "I'm afraid we've been a distasteful lot," he started, looking down at his heavy boots. "We've treated you badly, and we—we hope that you will be good enough to forgive us for our horrible behavior. Elisa and I—well, we are particularly grateful. As you know, Peter is doing well and will be home in a few more days from the hospital." He lifted his head with purpose and strode up to Jon to shake hands in a gesture of friendship. Jon took his hand, and even with his mangled use of the language, he acknowledged the group and nodded.

Elisa came forth lugging a beautiful handmade cradle. "I understand you will be needing this soon! And a few more things as well!" She motioned to the other women. They came forward with packages of all descriptions, and Flora felt her knees weaken and tears spring to her eyes. "Don't you speak, now, dear," chattered Elisa, taking Flora by the arm. "Clovis! What is taking you so long? There's a barn-raisin' to be done!" With that, they all laughed, and the men sprang to action, while the ladies smothered Flora with attention, piling into the house with their children, food, and gifts.

Jon's head spun and the blood coursed through his veins as he ushered the ladies into the house. As he at last turned to go in and change into his work clothes, he looked to the corral where Gustaf, Ilka, and Niss pressed against the rough corral poles to better see the extraordinary commotion. They ran in gay circles as if to celebrate the wondrous occasion, tossing their thick necks and whinnying a welcome to their brethren. "And crown thy good with brotherhood," Jon said aloud. America was truly the beautiful.

A Christmas Champ

Don't ever underestimate the power of the heart ...

"**W**ake up, Beck."

Beck opened her eyes to waning daylight slicing dark patches along the barn and a billowing cloud of dust working its way toward the open window of the pickup truck. As she slid erect, she turned to her dad in the driver's seat and shook her head. "There he goes again. Old Steeler's gonna buck him off for sure, this time." Becky sighed and looked back out at the young boy racing an imaginary timer in the arena beyond.

"Guess he's gotta try, hon," her father said with a half smile as he climbed out of the truck, watching his son and the ornery gray horse work their way around the fifty-five-gallon drums. Sam, her brother, brought the horse down to a trot and jogged over to where they were standing. He looked mighty pleased with himself and patted the horse on his damp, sweaty neck.

"Did you see, Dad? He's doing better all the time!" the boy said happily. Old Steeler just fixed his gaze on the barn and gave a horse-sized sigh. He'd been through a few kids, and this one was finally catching up, smarts-wise. It was just a matter of time and good weather, and they'd be packing him off to the local horse shows. Steeler shook himself all over and began to think better thoughts, thoughts about his dinner bucket waiting inside the barn and the peace and quiet the coming winter might provide.

76

Mac Gafferty had been a horse and pony veterinarian in Keene County for twenty-some years. He liked his work, and his occupation provided him contentedness and satisfaction. He was a man who thrived on the long, odd hours and strenuous work that accompanied the job. He had married later in life than most, and through his children he found the warmth and sparkle that his wife had left behind when she had died several years before. The Gaffertys lived moderately, and his many hours away from home had served to toughen the children to a rather systematic way of life, mostly owing to the small livestock operation they maintained. "Not for profit," he often told himself. "More for keeping things a bit busier for three energetic kids." Plenty of chores and a regular schedule sure kept dinner tasting better and bedtime more welcome.

Cherie was the eldest child and clearly the young homemaker in the family. She was nearly seventeen and had an endless array of projects going on at the local high school—she was a joiner, adept at social affairs, and the only one who didn't burn the eggs on Saturday mornings. Since Cherie did most of the housework, ten-year-old Sam and Becky, thirteen, spent their task time in the barns feeding, cleaning, and straightening up. All in all, it worked out just fine, because, while Sam would rather mow the grass, Becky would just as soon clean the stalls, and Cherie was purely relieved to be looking over the dishpan in the safety of the kitchen. They had a few head of horses: mostly for pleasure, sometimes for sale, and once in a while for makeshift cowponies—such as the time that their Hereford cow, Sashay, and her new calf had been found in the parking lot at the local shopping center, totally engrossed in sampling the spring sale on bedding plants. After the roundup, Sam had sat on his heaving horse, Steeler, and his eyes had played over the crowd of jovial shoppers pointing at the stock trailer where the exhausted Sashay lay with her baby, wearied by all of the chasing and commotion. "Think we'd better mosey on home now," he'd said. Doc Gafferty had agreed as he backed toward the trailer, apologizing the whole time to the disgruntled store manager—who kept looking down at the check freshly written to cover the damage of one hungry cow and her boisterous, clumsy calf.

Becky was Doc's assistant, and she loved to go along to the many farms on the call schedule. Spring was her favorite time for weekend and late-night excursions to the foaling sheds, where time and again she witnessed the birth of a newborn foal, each a champion in its own right for making the journey into the crisp, new world. Spring wormings, inoculations, and a never-ending list of routine and problem matters awaited Doc's red pickup truck, and Becky loved being a part of it all, doing her best to stay out of the way when she wasn't needed, running for the supplies when necessary, and learning the names and faces of the people and horses she'd met along the way. Summertime was especially great, because she could go more often during the weekday hours—unless, of course, an invitation to Betsy Johnson's pool was in the offing. "You mean to tell me you'd rather go swim and have some fun than come with me today?" her dad would ask with a smile, glad to see his daughter keeping her friends and other interests in proper perspective. Once in a while as they were dressing, Mac would say, "Not today, Becky—I've got lots of help," which usually meant he had an especially bad case or euthanasia to perform, not the nicest of sights and certainly hard on the heartstrings of owner and daughter alike.

The sun burned softly through the mid-October mist on what promised to be the beginning of a bright, cool day. It was a Saturday, and Dr. Gafferty loaded the truck with a few fresh items as Becky ran from the house to join him, munching on a warm muffin, compliments of sister Cherie. The first stop on the route was the Drew farm, where two geldings and a mare awaited the fall wormings. When the work was done, Dr. Gafferty graciously turned down the ever-present offer to stay for a cup of coffee. His attention turned to the next bit of business, a viral cough affecting the yearlings at the Bower Farm. This was an austere establishment of fine thoroughbreds located on the far side of the county. When they arrived, Ed Bower shouted a greeting from the confines of one of the barns, and Doc and Becky headed in the direction of his voice. Bower was a big man whose years showed in the deep lines on his face and whose rough manner belied the skill and ease with which he handled his horses. He took great pride in his thoroughbreds and always managed to get a visitor into his broodmare barn to show off his newest crop of colts and fillies. After examining the horses and starting antibiotic treatments, Doc lingered a moment to chat. "How are the mares doing, Ed?" he queried, and without fail, Mr. Bower ushered them over to where the mares were stalled, awaiting the months and days ahead as their due dates approached. They ended up in front of a roomy, beautiful stall, where a large black mare stood, heavy in foal to a popular sire of stakes winners. "She's a dandy, Mac," Ed said, his eyes roving over the slick mare as she nibbled hay.

"Yes, she sure is a fine gal, Ed," Mac replied.

"As I remember, she'll be due right on top of January, eh?"

"That's right, Doc," Ed replied. "It won't be long now, and I'm anxious to see what she'll have. First one for her—should be a right nice colt, 'least I'm hopin'. " They talked for a few more moments, and it was plain to see that Ed Bower was a very serious person when it came to breeding horseflesh, very serious indeed.

The next stop was the Jergens's place, where a horse needed some stitches removed. The quarter-horse gelding was still not too receptive to his patient status, however, and Mrs. Jergens was quite terrified of horses in general and this one in particular. "I'm not going to be of much help, as usual," she called from a respectable distance in the aisle, looking very worried as Doc struggled to calm the lunging animal. He managed to quiet the gelding, and Becky eased in with scissors and fresh bandages. Things went fairly smoothly from there, and a grateful Mrs. Jergens was jotting down final instructions for Mr. Jergens to follow. "How is Tommy's pony?" asked Doc, knowing her son and his undauntable affection for the aged pony mare in the pen outside. Tommy was Sam's age, and the two were forever discussing their adventures, much like two old-time cowboys reliving an embellished past.

"Just fine, Doctor," replied Mrs. Jergens. "Why, he'll pass up a pan of fresh-baked brownies just to shoot on out here after school and say hello to her. She certainly has been a good pal for that boy, I must say!" she said, smiling. Doc agreed, wished them well, and he and Becky headed the truck back out onto the road. The calls went on into early evening, and at last the day was over.

The days rolled by through November as autumn leaves blew about the stripped trees, and the hint of snow came whistling on the ear-nipping gusts. A call came in from the Jergens early in the morning on a blustery day. "Can you stop by—it's the pony mare, and she's bad off." Mac hurried over to their barn, where the little mare stood stiffly in her stall. "Foundered, I think," Mr. Jergens said. "She'd gotten to the corn bin and must have spent the better part of the night with her head in it."

Doc examined the mare, who was beginning to experience the painful sensations in her feet and who was reluctant to budge as a result of her digestive overload. "She's going to get worse," Doc said as he injected a dose of bute to fight the inflammation. "It's coming on fast, and I'm afraid it is going to be serious. Get some buckets full of ice water and get her feet soaking. Put her on straight grass hay and water, and we'll hope for the best."

As he left with instructions for the pony's care and a promise to return, he passed little Tommy and put his hand on the boy's head. Tommy sat lifelessly on a bale of hay, filled with shame and guilt. "I didn't latch the door, sir," he began in a quavering voice. "I forgot to lock it, and she got into the corn. I made her real sick. " He looked up at Doc with liquid eyes. "Will she be okay?"

Doc looked past the boy's small frame to the stall. "Let's see what tomorrow brings, all right? We'll do the best we can, and you can help." Tommy dropped his head again as Doc left, his shoulders beginning to quake with held-back sobs.

The ensuing days brought no relief to the pony, who bore the agonizing effects of acute laminitis. When she stood, the pain in her hooves caused her to keep her hind legs well under her and her front end suspended gingerly on her heels. Her bright, inquisitive attitude dropped to a glazed expression of pain, and it was apparent that her system was losing ground in the progression of the disease. One day, she collapsed wearily and would not arise. Her age and the severity of the laminitis brought the decision to put her to sleep. With sadness for the boy, Doc made his final visit, leaving only her memory upon his departure. The mare would hurt no more.

Weeks slipped by, and Christmastime was fast approaching. Ice appeared on the glistening water buckets, and everyone seemed cheery for the festiveness of the holiday season. Evenings brought glowing lights from decorated homes, and sprigs of evergreens peeked out from beneath car trunks and truck beds. Packages were secretly wrapped, and holiday ware traveled down attic stairs to embellish mantels and windowsills, while the white, stark land bore symbols of gaiety wherever one looked.

Just three days before Christmas, Mr. Bowers put in an urgent call for

Mac. His black mare had begun delivery of her foal. By the time Becky and Doc arrived, the mare had proceeded with the birth in a normal fashion, producing a very dark, very small foal with a couple of white socks, who was busy keeping his head off the deep straw while trying to figure out just what in blazes had dumped him there. Mr. Bowers, instead of being happy with the situation, was quite red in the face and walked to and from the scene with growing disgust. It took a while for the story to come out, but, after Doc calmed the man down, he learned why Mr. Bowers was so upset. He'd recently discovered that, in a bizarre and accidental way, at the breeding farm where he'd taken his mare, she had been put into a pasture with an Appaloosa stud pony that they used for a teaser stallion. Ed Bowers was absolutely sure that the foal belonged not to his well-touted racehorse Daddy, but to the Appaloosa. "Just because he's small, Ed—" Doc began to say.

But Bowers cut him off quickly with, "Look at his feet, there, Mac! Look at his eyes and his muzzle! He's a baby, but there ain't no thoroughbred I ever seen with strippity-striped hooves and a marble muzzle. No, sirree!—that's no colt of mine! And he ain't going to stay, either! I have a reputation to think of! I want this foal put down. "

After examining the little colt and afterbirth, and after administering iodine to the baby's navel, Doc pushed back his cap and stood. It certainly was unusual, he agreed, and even the black mare hung back skeptically. She wasn't quite sure yet just what she had produced; she was not the seasoned veteran that her broodmare friends in the neighboring stalls were. She tentatively nosed her foal and began to lick it, permanently forming the bond between mother and foal. Becky watched and cheered inside for the mare, whose attention was now focused entirely upon her colt as she nuzzled it and whose rough tongue continued to follow its course on the baby, whose head bobbed with every nudge.

Doc and Becky drove home quietly, and as Becky stared out of the window, she felt an anger rise within. "I heard you talking, Dad," she said, "And it's not fair! You're not going to go back there and—" She stopped, at loss for the words to follow.

"I don't want to, Becky," Mac replied. "But it could happen with or without my help. We'll have to wait and see what happens. I have to do what I have to do sometimes." Becky felt sick to her stomach, and was happy to see their driveway in sight.

The next evening, a call came from Mr. Bowers, and Mac took it in his office at home. He stood up and closed the door. He then talked for quite a while before he came out, slipped his cap on, and told the kids he would be gone for a few hours. He would not meet the hard stares of Becky or Sam, nor would he allow company on his journey that evening. He said he had to run an errand and then visit a client. As he left, Becky picked up a couch pillow and flung it to the floor. Sam did the same. "He's going to do it," Becky spat, eyes and mouth set in a hard line.

"Can't let it happen," Sam said with Billy-the-Kid determination.

Becky looked at him. "Just what are we going to do about it?" she said with uncontrolled sarcasm.

At that moment, Cherie entered the room. After looking at the pair she commented, "If that's your best Season's Greeting tonight, you'd better put in an order to Santa for a couple of smiling faces—what's eating you two?"

In a moment, Cherie was bombarded with the atrocity of the situation in a short, explosive, kid-cussing explanation from Becky and Sam. Cherie's face darkened in sympathy, and she agreed that it certainly didn't seem fair. Sam brightened and he said, "Cherie, you can help—we CAN do something!"

Cherie listened and then shook her head in a "no-way-you-are-stark-raving-mad" fashion. "We can't go over there and steal that mare and foal out of that barn! Even if we could get away with it—it's just impossible, and I'm not being any part of any nutty scheme to spirit off a mare and colt out of someone else's barn, no way!"

She turned, and Sam and Becky jumped to her sides. "Just drive us," they pleaded. "We won't tell a soul, and no one will know you did it—you've got to help us!" After a period of arm-tugging, old-secret threatening, and New Year's bribes, Cherie grabbed her coat and her car keys and said, "You guys are going to get me into a bunch of trouble! And this is something

I'd never do in a million years—better call me Clarice, because I am NOT Cherie Gafferty tonight!" With that, they dashed out the door to rescue the foal.

The would-be horse thieves arrived twenty minutes later to the dark, windswept farm with a sign swinging animatedly over the gate: Bower Farm. Becky and Sam jumped out of the car and left Cherie fingering her necklace with the golden cross and muttering a string of sinister comments about the consequences. "Looks like we got here in time!" Becky whispered as they crept toward the big broodmare barn. "No one around, and they keep their dogs inside at night."

"The door is locked!" Sam hissed, so they slipped around the barn to the side where the mares' stalls were.

"Some lights on by the stalls; let's take a look! C'mon, Sam, get on my shoulders, and get up and take a look!" Becky said softly.

Sam clambered roughly up above the groans escaping Becky and looked through the first window. "Wrong stall—bay horse." They moved one closer to where Becky remembered the horse to be. "Gray mare." Once more they moved down to where another soft glow reached the evening darkness. "Empty," Sam said.

"Empty?" Becky questioned. "I'm sure she was between a gray and a chestnut. Let's go to the next. "

Sam looked for a long moment. "Chestnut," he said uneasily. "And there's only one more."

"Let's see," said Becky.

As she exerted another mighty effort, she heard from over her head, ""Bay. Bay with a star."

"Get down; you're breaking my back!" Becky spouted and then dumped Sam on the hard, cold ground. With that, they pondered the unthinkable— they were too late.

They walked back to the road in the soft snow and jogged to where Cherie waited skittishly in the car. "Well?" she asked nervously. "What's going on?" Becky and Sam gave their discouraged reply, and they rode home in silence. Everyone went to bed with a heavy heart, and not a one left the light on for Dad.

Christmas morning dawned in homes across the land with the warm significance of the day at hand. At the breakfast table, before church, talk was nil, and when Doc appeared with a hearty greeting he was met with something less than holly-bright hellos. Between post-breakfast coffee and the last of the chores outside, the glum mood prevailed. Mac finally rounded up the three children and sat them down in the kitchen. "Now— what is it?" Cold silence hung in the air, but it was finally pierced by Sam, who in no uncertain terms told his father just what the problem was. His sentences were interrupted by outbursts from Becky, and as Mac listened, he sat back and gave each of them a solemn look. When quiet once more prevailed, everyone's gaze was fixed on either the toaster or the floor or the icebox. Mac spoke evenly. "I'll talk to you all in good time about what has to be and what doesn't have to be. I can understand your feelings about this, but what you did was wrong—capital W! Wrong for you and possibly very damaging to me. Now, get yourselves dressed, because we are going to church and then to your cousin's house for dinner." With that, he left them and set about finishing up the last of the chores.

The church was filled, and the last hymn rang out in a joyful chorus that led to a lot of hand-shaking and kissing and good, long hugs from neighbors and friends. The Gafferty family loaded into the car, and when Mac drove to the Jergens's farm, no one even asked why. *Couldn't these doctoring calls even wait one day for Christmas?* Doc got out, stood next to the car, and motioned Cherie to roll down the window. "Are you all planted in there like poinsettias, or what? Let's go!" he said, and they all trudged to the small turnout behind the Jergens's barn. The colt was still unsteady on his tiny, stilt-like legs, but he'd found his momma's rich treasures and spent his waking moments walking around her and nursing. Becky's eyes nearly popped out of her head as she drank in the picture before her, while Sam was bent frozen between two rails of the board fence. Cherie just gazed adoringly at her father and smiled as if to say she'd known all along.

Doc spoke. "I had to do a whole lot of talking to get this done," he said, "and when I tried to convince Ed Bower that he was better off letting the mare have her first baby by her side for at least four months, he didn't want anything to do with the idea. Pride, you see. But there's a boy in that house that can use something to keep him real busy right now, and this colt is going to be needing a good home as well. I don't mind saying that it was the hardest doctorin' speech I ever had to give, and I just want you to know," he said, looking them all straight in the eye, "that if something happens to this mare in the next few months while she's here, you're all going to be on sweeper's wages. And one other thing—not a word about any of this to anyone!" With that, one of the Jergens's barn cats jumped squarely to the top of Doc's battered cap from its perch on the fence. "Sure hard to give a serious lecture around here," said Doc just as Tommy came running from the house. His joy was hard to miss as he long-slid to a stop on the icy ground.

"Isn't he just something?" he grinned. "I named him Lucky, 'cause Dad and Mom said I don't know how lucky we are to have him. He's going to be the best horse anywhere!" Sam lobbed a snowball at Tommy, and they ran laughing into the yard beyond. Mrs. Jergens appeared and said sternly, "Mac Gafferty—you march yourself into that house for a cup of coffee and some homemade Christmas cake! You're not getting away this time!"

With that, the girls grabbed Mac, and they walked to the house arm in arm, heart in heart.

One Christmas Knight

The ground was gravelly and unyielding where I pounded my fists in a fit of anger and frustration. I sat back and stared at the back of my truck. Katie, my mare, shuffled her feet in the trailer, jarring the rig gently as I rocked back on my haunches and peered at the broken rear axle hanging limply and uselessly on the gravel beside the roadway. With a whoosh and whir of rubber on cement, a car sped by, and then another, hauling their busy occupants to destinations unknown to me on this miserable, damp October day.

My hands hurt where the stones had pressed into them. I heaved myself back into the truck and stared ahead to the horizon now thickening in the gloom as dusk settled in. I couldn't stop the tears then, and they flowed freely as I wrapped my arms around the steering wheel. I buried my face in my arms and sobbed like a child at my predicament. Nothing was fair in my life—nothing was easy! It might have been minutes or hours that passed, when I was startled by a rap at my window. I awoke from my daze to see a young man's face there, tousled hair spilling from beneath a red woolen cap, his breath steaming in the cold air of twilight. "Can I help?" he asked, and I stared at him, but then I wiped my streaked face with a greasy hand and opened the door. I sighed, "I don't really see how," and I motioned to the rear end of the truck.

Katie whinnied loudly and impatiently and her seven-month-old filly reiterated the demand. "Out!" they demanded of me.

"I'm afraid I am in quite a jam here. My truck is broken, and it's such a lonely road, with no houses in sight to call for help," I said. *Fat chance, anyhow*, I thought to myself. I didn't have a dime on me to make the call or tow the truck even if I did get to a phone—it was that kind of day.

The young fellow pursed his lips and nodded. "Where were you headed, anyway?" he asked. I told him where I was going. "Twelve miles or so? Well, we'd better get moving; it's getting pretty late," he said.

"But—how?" I queried, seeing no vehicle whatsoever from which the lad had alighted.

"When life hands you lemons, make lemonade. I'd say a dozen legs should get us there," he replied, and with that, he walked around and unfastened the trailer door. Katie gladly backed out, and her filly stood in the doorway for a moment before taking a giant leap onto the shoulder of the road. With lead shanks in hand, we began our slow journey home to the rhythmic clip-clop of the horses' hooves and a playful filly tugging at her lead.

We walked along for a while, until finally my manners reappeared. I thanked him for his help and asked him his name. "Whelp," he said with a serious pose, "my whole name is Maximillian Beauregard Riley III, but you can call me Max, if you please, milady. Sir Max of the Round Table and guardian of fair damsels in distress. "

Fair I was not, but the distress part fit like an old shoe, so I had to grin and return the bow. "And you, kind sir, may call me Josie, Queen of Scots, flats, and busted axles!" It was quite easy to talk to Max, and as we walked on, I guess I must have poured out my whole life's story. He was patient as he listened to all of it, including my day's discretions, which included being fired from my part-time job.

"Got the old pink slip today," I explained. I had been working at a fancy show barn, partially to pay for the board there for my mare and foal and partially because the additional salary helped pay expenses on my mortgage. I had a small house and five acres that I was trying hard to hold onto after my divorce of some years back.

"What happened?" Max asked.

"It was so dumb!" I replied, blushing at the remembrance of the circumstances of the afternoon.

"I had turned out this very expensive gelding, as I usually do every day, and I didn't realize that his pen was adjacent to a newcomer, a yearling colt, who then chewed his tail off up to his—well, the owner was fit to be tied when she got there, and I was sent packing, horses and all. "

Max caught my glum expression and then laughed. "Oh boy, I'll bet she was hot!" he said.

Hot just wasn't the word, I thought to myself. "Hot?" I said. "She was foaming at the mouth and stamping her Givenchys in the dirt so hard I thought they'd split! John, my boss, well, he was apologizing right and left, stammering and fussing over her like a mother hen—and there that fancy old show horse stood looking like his butt had the tail of a … showy Belgian!"

I shook my head and smiled a bit then, mostly because I was just so sick of feeling lousy over it. "Enough of my tales of woe!" I exclaimed. "What about yours?"

Max glanced back to the now-tired and docile filly and then to me. "Mine?" he said. "Right now, it's you," and with that we had entered the long, bumpy driveway up to the little house and barn that I called home.

"Now, here is the last problem of the day," I said as I tugged at the old, squeaky door on the barn, which was really just a rickety old shed but a temporary shelter that would have to suffice for my mare and foal. One grubby light bulb gave off a dingy yellow glow as I surveyed the floor and began to clear out the miscellaneous junk that had been scattered about for years. I managed to find a few buckets for water, and we put the horses in so Katie could inspect her new quarters. She sniffed her dark dwelling with a marked air of disdain, and her large, liquid eyes queried mine for her soft straw bed and manger full of feed. "Sorry, gal," I said quietly, thinking of the bales of alfalfa we had left behind on my truck. "Fix you up in the morning, hey?" I filled the buckets with water and left.

Max followed me up to the house and I once again apologized, as I always did, for the shaky stairs and the peeling paint. The house, like the shed, had seen better days.

Max stopped me in midsentence. "Shush, child! Why, it's as bonnie a castle as I've ever laid eyes on!" He ushered me in with a flourish of hands and a twinkling grin. I smiled at his dauntless good humor and offered him a cup of coffee to chase the chill away. He declined firmly and said, "Must go--I sure wish you good luck," and with that he hopped down from the stoop and was gone, his tireless legs carrying him easily across my yard. As he disappeared, I watched with a strange feeling of loss. In the few hours we had spent together, I had felt somehow that I knew him—and that there was something disturbing about Max and that wonderful smile.

I called in sick to my regular job the next day, so I could organize the barn, which so sadly lacked for equine graces, and to make the necessary arrangements for my truck and the trailer to be brought home. With the help of a borrowed pickup truck, I begged the local auto repair shop for speedy recovery of my own truck and then returned the horse trailer to my old workplace and John, my old boss, who greeted me with a sad, tired look.

"I'm really sorry to lose you, Josie," he said. "You've been a great employee and hard to replace. You can understand, though, I'm sure. "

I said yes, I did understand, and I thanked the man who had always treated me kindly and fairly. "I'll sure miss you, too," I said and then drove away with a heavy heart.

I felt even worse when I returned home. Katie and her foal nickered and neighed for their feed, and as I surveyed the deteriorating barn, I felt a deepening despair. I had no place to turn them out, and they simply could not stay locked up for long. A pile of posts I'd purchased the summer before lay nearby, but it seemed an insurmountable task. With winter closing in, the ground would soon be frozen solid. I had just the weekends to work, and the pen would have to wait for spring, even if the horses couldn't. I dug out some tools and string, determined to at least start the task. I did not know what else to do.

Weeks went by quickly, and still my horses waited impatiently for some relief from their gloomy walls. I led them by hand as much as I could, but my frustration grew daily along with my calluses and chapped lips from the cold evening air. I'd managed to get half the posts in, a long way from finishing, and it seemed like forever since I'd begun. Thanksgiving was nearly here, and I looked forward to having the extra days to use for putting the last posts in the ground.

One day when I came home from work, I was astounded to find the last post in, securely tamped, and ready for wire. The skeletal frame of the new corral was in place against the stark November treescape. I suddenly realized that no whinny had greeted me—unusual for this late feeding hour. I rushed over to the little shed and opened the door—to find the horses bedded deeply in fresh straw and munching contentedly on their dinner. The cobwebs had been brushed away and the light bulb replaced with a shiny new fixture. I stood there staring about, and the tap on my shoulder made me jump. I turned to see Max, youthful grin and bemused eyes greeting mine. "Not exactly a slain dragon, milady, but progress in the Black Forest, anyway! I'll take you up on the hot brew now, if the offer still stands!" I gratefully obliged.

I studied Max as he drank his coffee and found myself wondering about his age. He was so young, yet with wisdom beyond his age. He was not a child or a man, but he had qualities of both. As I pondered this ambiguity, I stared down at my worn hands and felt much older and dowdier than I had in a long time. Max stayed for dinner that night and then left as mysteriously as he had arrived, and on foot once again. He jogged away into the blackness of night. My curiosity was equaled only by my gratitude, however, and I retired sleepily with the long-forgotten comfort of feeling cared for.

The weeks sped by quickly. Max came nearly every day, and I would come home to find him busy with some chore or another or with brushing the mare and her robust filly. "Doesn't she have a name?" he asked one day as he toiled over the filly.

I shook my head. "No, I can't seem to think of one that fits her," I replied. "Any ideas?"

"No," Max said, "I'm sure one will come to you."

We turned them out in their new corral, and with delight we watched them whirl and spin and circle their new domain, tails aloft in the cool air, winter coats glistening under Max's firm grooming. Sometimes Max would take them in hand for long, long treks under the December sun, and stride for stride they would go across the brown winter ground, leaping and racing. Max delighted in this play. He ran and ran until I thought his legs would fall off, but he seemed to take a special privilege in it all. I promised Max I would teach him to ride, but he said he was just happy to be around the horses. I felt a deep bond developing between Max and my filly, and, more tentatively, between Max and me.

"I'm too old to feel this way," I told myself, and even in denial, a smile would cross my lips as I thought of Max. I thanked him silently in my prayers every day—for the warmth, the companionship, and the unceasing help he provided.

I learned to look forward to each day again, I dressed better, and my sense of well-being returned. One day I came home to find Max way up high in a tree, perched there like a spring songbird. "What in the world are you doing?" I asked.

He replied, "Just wanted to see what it was like!"

"Haven't you ever climbed a tree before?" I laughed.

"Nope--but I like it!" he shouted back. He clambered down, and we retired to the house for dinner. The house was looking better these days. Together we had scraped and painted and pounded in loose nails and it looked quite cozy with its cap of snow. Christmas was fast approaching, upon the whitened boughs of the evergreens and in the gleaming stars of the December night. I knew I had to get Max a very special gift, and I lay awake thinking of just such a present. Nothing in the stores appealed to me, and I grew frustrated as the day approached. My little tree, decorated so brightly, was a very cheerful sight, but as the packages beneath its multicolored branches grew in number, I realized that the most important one was still missing. I decided that only something handmade would do for Max, so I purchased a piece of fine leather with which to make him a vest. I could still sew a little and I knew that it would be, if not the most extravagant gift he received, the most lovingly created. I worked deep into the nights on it, adding a scarf to accentuate the rich, soft patina of the leather. Finally, upon its completion, I added a note: Josie and the Girls. I wrapped it and set it beneath the tree.

Christmas Eve arrived, and I spent the evening at home with a few of my friends, keeping a watchful eye on the door for Max to appear. When he didn't arrive by nine o'clock, my vigil waned, with the knowledge that he would not appear. After my last guest had left, I put my jacket on and trekked restlessly out to the barn, disappointment biting at me with each stride. I turned on the light to greet my horses, and spotted the beautifully ribboned package laid carefully next to Katie's stall. I sat down on a bale of hay and opened it. Inside was an oil portrait of my beloved mare and her filly, captured expertly in a breathtaking pose, and exquisitely painted. What an incredibly handsome portrait! In the corner were the initials MBRIII and the words To Lady Josie, with the date.

On Christmas Day, I waited again for Max, and again I was terribly disappointed at his absence. On a chance, I took out the phone book and looked up the name Riley and was surprised and relieved to find a listing in the book. As darkness set in, I warmed up the truck and took off into a neighboring town to find the address, my present for Max on the seat alongside me. I drove to the address, where I spied a stately home nestled within a black wrought-iron fence, with two beautiful wreaths adorning the double doors. I stood there hesitantly on the snowy landing and then timidly knocked on the big brass doorknocker with the fancy engraved *R*.

A woman answered the door. I smiled and greeted her, and I motioned to the gift beneath my arm. "Is Max here?" I asked hopefully. "I wanted to give him a Christmas present."

The woman in the doorway stared hard at me, and for a moment, I thought she might become ill. Her lips opened, but no sound came forth. She motioned for me to wait as she disappeared through a hallway. I felt quite uncomfortable, but then I became preoccupied with the paintings on the wall of the gracious foyer. They were of different breeds of horses, some with riders, some without, but all were beautifully detailed scenes and easily recognizable as the work of Max.

Just then a fatherly looking man appeared and acknowledged my presence. "Would you come with me?" he asked, and I followed him up a staircase to a room down the hall. "I'd like to show you Max's room," he said, and he opened the door. Once inside, I gazed upon the bedroom and its walls filled with mementos and paraphernalia. I stepped closer. A row of porcelain horses stood stately on a shelf, and awards and ribbons were pinned carefully to the relics of the past. A state university banner hung beside the dresser, and I noticed an assortment of photographs upon the desk. One picture was taken as a sports event of some kind, and Max proudly held a large golden trophy, his unmistakable grin accompanying the victoriously raised fist. I peered at all of the other photos as well, and I looked back at his father in the doorway with the obvious question on my lips. Max was wheelchair bound in each and every photo.

As he closed the door behind us, Max's father turned to look at me with heavy eyes and an expression of an old sadness mixed in with compassion. "This isn't the first time this has happened," he started. "My boy has been … gone … for three years now. Once in a while we hear from someone like you who he has been in contact with …" His voice trailed off, and although I felt faint, I managed to keep a sturdy profile. Somehow the strength came to me to reach out and touch Mr. Riley's hand in a gesture of understanding and acceptance, even though the rest of me reeled in agonizing perception.

"I'm going to miss him," I whispered. "Your son was the most special gift I'll ever receive." We walked down the stairs together, and at the bottom of the steps, I paused and looked up to see a painting of a mare and foal galloping across a snow-spattered pasture, running for the pure joy of it. "I have a filly like that," I said slowly. "Her name is Maxie."

With that, I walked out the door into the Christmas night. The stars in the clear black sky were never brighter and the blessing from above never stronger.

"Merry Christmas, Max," I said softly. " I will ride for you, and I will run for you, and I will never forget you."

Somewhere Between Christmas and Yesterday

It was in Portland, Oregon, in the late spring of the year before the Rose Festival consumed the city in the sweet aura of fresh blossoms and splashing color. Two women stood before the poster in the hotel lobby. "Oh, Maggie—we'd have to rent a car, and I really had wanted to do some shopping over on the coast tomorrow. Do you really want to drive all that way to see a rodeo?"

"Yes, I think I do," Maggie said thoughtfully as she continued to gaze at the advertisement before her. "But don't worry about me; you go on ahead and buy out all the shops, and I'll just go alone, if you don't mind. I might meet a handsome cowboy, and who knows—you might find your West Coast millionaire!" They giggled and walked on, chatting about their accommodations and discussing their plans for the days ahead. With the convention coming up, the women had much to do while they were in the Northwest, and the time would go by quickly.

The next day, as the sun nodded lazily past the Cascades on its journey to the ocean, the rental car slid past telephone poles and miles of forested beauty, dotted here and there with ranches and small towns whose sudden appearance woke Maggie up from her deep thoughts. She pulled into the grounds of the rodeo, nestled neatly into the foot of a jagged range, and she stepped out of the car. Almost immediately she felt the old butterflies begin to stir—but along with the excitement came a sense of foreboding and a feeling of something terribly wrong. Maggie took a deep breath and put those thoughts aside, as she was determined to do, and she began to mosey into the stream of Western hats funneling into the stands. A medley of cowboy tunes was blaring over the loudspeakers as she stood close to the fence and watched the horses and riders warming up in the spacious arena. She was very conscious of her in-town clothing and leather pumps and thought wryly, "I must look like a real city slicker. No boots, no hat, no horse!" She shook her head and then wandered around to the back of the bleachers to see the contestants preparing for their events. The barrel racers, dressed in pretty Western shirts and silver belt buckles, trotted and loped their lithe mounts as the ropers picked through their rope cans and shook out loops. The rough-stock riders leaned back on trailers and stretched near truck beds, spurs in place, mentally tuning up for their rides to come. As the darkness blotted the sun's last rays, her eyes rested upon a bald-faced bay tied to a stock trailer.

"Bonner," she whispered, "it is you, isn't it, boy?" The horse picked up his eyes and ears momentarily, and after her trailing fingers left his neck he cocked his hip and returned to his waiting.

"Excuse me, ma'am," came a voice from behind her, and a lean cowboy carrying his gear approached the gelding and began to saddle him. Maggie stepped back and, finally, as the cowboy was buckling on the skid boots, she asked, "Is this horse's name Bonner? I mean, does he belong to a man named Lance Keater?"

"Ma'am?" replied the cowboy, glancing back at Maggie. "The horse belongs to me, but, yes, I did buy him from Skeet about three years ago." He stood and looked long and hard at Maggie. She quickly thanked him and began to turn away as the unasked question spilled from his lips. "You looking for him? He's over there, about to get up on Yellowbear." He cocked his head in the direction of the bucking chutes, and Maggie turned to see the last of the grand entry reappear from their colorful parade before the eager crowd. In moments, the first bareback horse would emerge. Maggie felt her courage ebb away with each step as she made her way to the chutes and the flurry of activity surrounding them.

The big yellow bronc gazed with little interest from between the boards as the bareback rig was placed on his back and cautiously snugged up beneath his belly. An old contender, he reserved his energies for the time when the gate swung wide and he would be released to vent his distrust and violence in the dirt beyond. The bareback riders were lined up behind the chutes doing their warm-up rituals, and the tall one whose name had been chosen for the yellow horse stood up and pulled his glove on, browned and blackened from untold rides and rosin. "Make a ride, Skeet!" hollered a stocky man from above the number-four chute. "You drew good—this one ought to be in the bank for the all-around!" As Skeet straddled the wood and began to lower himself upon the rough hide of the bronc, he paused. From the loudspeaker came the score of the last rider, and as they were announcing his name, the faintest smell of perfume caught Skeet's nostrils. It was unmistakable in the pungent mixture of horseflesh and leather and humid sweat. Skeet heard nothing then, and his head jerked around as the scent lingered. Suddenly he called, "Turn him out," and then he jumped down from the boards to disappear in the dimness. "What, are you crazy?" the chute man returned. "Skeet, get back on this horse—Skeet!" With a shake of his hat and a bewildered frown, the man motioned to the gate man—and, with that, the yellow bronc named Yellowbear bucked out riderless, roughly celebrating his empty victory.

When Maggie entered the bar, she knew he'd be there, parked at the far table, sitting alone with a half-empty glass. She approached him from behind and softly called his name. For a moment, Skeet did nothing to acknowledge her presence. Then, slowly, he pivoted on his chair. As his eyes met hers, there was a momentary softening and then a hardening of his expression. "Hello, Maggie." They paused there in silence, until at last she moved past him and sat down.

"Skeet, I came here to find you, but I don't know why, and I don't know what to say." She searched for the words as her eyes examined the lines and creases in the face before her.

He lit a cigarette without moving his gaze and said quietly, "Why did you leave? Just tell me now; it doesn't matter anymore."

"Oh, Skeet, it was so many years ago. I've tried to tell myself that it was the right thing to do, that it was what had to be, but I never meant to hurt you. I suppose that I wanted you to know that, and maybe that's why I'm here."

Skeet said, "Maggie, it was so good then. When you left, a big part of me went with you and never came back. And here you are now, for whatever reason. Hell—you never even said good-bye."

They talked for a while in awkwardness, pulling thoughts and words from dark pockets in their memories as the jukebox played country music and soft, sad ballads to accentuate the darkness and the pain. "There's a stocking-legged colt up off the highway just outside of town," Skeet said with a strained grin. "Every time I see the thing I can't help but think of you. You always liked a good-looking black horse."

"That part of my life is over," Maggie replied quietly. "I've got a life and a home now back East, and I'll be leaving in a day or so. I'm sorry, but I just don't know how to—"

He interrupted her in an abrupt push away from the table for two and stood to leave. "You go ahead, Maggie. I guess I should say good-bye this time, but I can't." He turned to leave and then stopped to face her once again. "I guess I just wish they'd get rid of that damned colt up the road, is all." With that, he strode away, and as she watched him walk out of the door, the sting in Maggie's eyes turned to tears. She was grateful for the corner and the shadows and for the obscurity of being a stranger.

Months passed, and the summer greens faded to brown and then fell to earth as the cold winds swept them away. Maggie buried herself in her work, and when the walls of her apartment grew small and threatened to close in upon her, she took long walks in the brisk air. A restlessness was growing within her, and she tried to shake off those feelings, as she had done once before. She had to get back to living the life that she had made for herself. Even the aroma of roasting turkeys and the sound of ringing bells over Thanksgiving failed to arouse any cheer, and instead of looking forward to the Christmas break in her schedule, Maggie felt the chill of trepidation as the day approached. *It took me a long, long time to feel comfortable here*, she thought to herself, *and now, after all this time, I'm still torn by old memories.*

Angered by her helplessness, she spent more and more time at the office and took work home so she wouldn't notice the colorful lights and the city in song, busily preparing for the celebrations ahead. Just a week before Christmas, Maggie was offered the opportunity to travel to California for a holiday show of southwestern design in fabric. Those with families in the company had no desire to travel at that time, so she gladly took the assignment. A change of scenery would do her good, she felt, and it might lift her out of the depression she was suffering through. When Maggie arrived in San Bernardino, she was indeed feeling more chipper for a change, and she even felt caught up in the festiveness of the decorations about town. After seeing to her business, she was free to roam around for the rest of the week, poking through the many beautiful shops in the area. One day, late into the week, she returned to her hotel room to see a bottle of chilled champagne resting on the table. She picked up the note and read, "Compliments of the Management. Merry Christmas!" Maggie dropped the note to the floor and sat down upon the bed as she stared at the two plastic glasses next to the champagne. She began to cry. At last her tears ran freely, and then they ran out. When morning arrived, Maggie was gone, and the untouched bottle stood silent testimony to her flight in the still of the darkened room.

The gray clouds hung heavily over the mountains on Christmas morning as Skeet slung his well-worn saddle over the back of the stout sorrel colt, whose spine humped up as he tightened the girth. After leading the horse off a few steps, Skeet cheeked him and stepped up lightly into the saddle. The gelding stood stock-still for a split second, and as Skeet pulled his rein around, the horse began to pitch and fight for his head, jumping stiffly in the cold air. In a short time, Skeet had the colt traveling in wide circles, blowing some, but ready for a day's work. He headed him out between the sagging gateposts and loped off into the hills, which were yet untouched by winter's storm. There were cattle still up in hidden ravines and wooded thickets, whose offspring had eluded the last search, and Skeet prepared to gather what he could before the weather made it difficult to round them up. The absence of the glitter and laughter of that special day was soothing to him, and the quiet of the valley gave him a source of peace. As he jogged along, he remembered a Christmas Day long ago, and although the outrage was gone, the memory prevailed. It was the day that Maggie had left. Like a maverick calf, she had bolted, and at long last, he could abandon the search.

Miles away, at the Corvallis Airport, Maggie appeared from the ladies' room, leaving behind a neatly stacked pile of clothing on the floor. As she walked, she felt the unaccustomed snugness of jeans and heard the old familiar click of boot-heels on the sharply polished floor as she headed for the man and the waiting truck outside the terminal. "Beau! It's so good to see you!" she exclaimed, and she handed him her bags. He threw them in the back, and they stepped into the cab of the pickup truck.

"Well, it's awfully good to see you, too," he said, glancing over. "I can't really believe you're back. I probably should mind my own business and shouldn't ask what your plans are, but, like I told you on the phone, you're welcome to use my rig. Headin' west, are you?"

"Yes," Maggie replied, "I've got some unfinished business to take care of." After a moment, she said, "Beau, I'm so grateful to you. You know, it's been hard for me, too, but it's time for me to start over. I hope I'm not too late."

"Don't worry your pretty head about that," Beau laughed with a knowing smile, and Maggie grinned at the compliment and at his confidence. They drove past the outskirts of town, and soon Beau pulled into his home driveway and to the house ahead, skillfully wheeling truck and horse trailer through the yard and then pointing it back out to the road. From inside, several tousled heads appeared, peeking through the brightly lit boughs of a Christmas tree within. As Beau said good-bye, he squeezed Maggie's hands in his. "Welcome back, kid," he said, and with that she took the wheel and drove away.

A half an hour later, she slowed to read the sign swinging high above the ranch posts, and then she pulled into a drive where the barn lights illuminated a fellow who was busy throwing bales of hay down from the barn loft to the floor. "Hello," she called out and then got out of the truck to introduce herself. She motioned into the field by the road with firm intent. The man scratched his head, and after a bit of negotiation, he nodded, and they shook gloved hands in the damp air.

It was late in the afternoon when Skeet headed his small heard of ornery cattle off the slick side of the mountain and to the pass below. It was difficult to keep them lined out in the moist, chilly air with darkness settling in, but his weary horse moved out at the touch of a spur to turn the occasional renegade back to the herd, and at last the group was within sight of the small ranch house and waiting corral. When Skeet was close enough to the ranch, his eyes picked out a lone horse pacing the fence in his roping pen, and as he squinted to see better, he also spotted the truck and trailer parked in the shadow of the barn. "Beau!" he said out loud. "Now, I wonder what he'd be up to today." He quickened his pace and soon had the cows and their calves milling about the feed bunks, secure in their new quarters. He trotted his horse back to the roping pen and stared at the white-legged colt in the pen, whose ink-black coat was throwing steam and who was plainly unhappy about being alone in a strange corral. Skeet's brow creased in confusion—until he saw her on the opposite side of the pen, and suddenly the realization hit him.

He waited until Maggie climbed the gate and walked over the hard ground to where he was sitting on the sorrel. She put her foot up and stood on the second rail of the fence to address him. She cleared her throat and began, "I hear you break colts for people now and then. I wonder if you'd break mine."

He pushed his hat back a notch and gave her a half smile. "You know," he said, "it takes a while to get them rode. Months—sometimes even years. I'd like to think that my customers might look in on them now and then while they're getting their education."

"Well, if that's all part of the deal," Maggie said, "then let's get started right away." She pulled herself up and over the fence. "Skeet, I'm hoping it will take forever."

Skeet stepped down from his horse, and they stood in silence before one another as the years of loneliness and heartache evaporated like the steamy breath of the horse at their side. "Merry Christmas, Maggie. Welcome home." They embraced and gave one other the most precious gift of all— each other.

The Best One Yet

Sometime around the turn of the century ...

Mattie and Helen chatted and sipped hot, fresh coffee from the comfort of Mattie's large, old-fashioned farm kitchen, until their talk was disrupted by lively, loud conversation stabbing into the kitchen from the sitting room. Helen rolled her eyes and set her cup down on the clothed oaken table. She groaned, "Lands' sakes, just one moment of peace. Is that too much to ask?" Mattie glumly nodded in agreement. It wasn't often that the sisters had the time or opportunity to visit with each other, and each moment was a pleasant break from the ordinary.

Beyond the door of the kitchen, Emmett and Sylvester escalated their quarrel into a heated argument. Mattie rose, closed the door with a decided *thud*, and returned to pour another cup of steaming brew. "You'd think by now that those horses would be a dull subject!" she spouted. Helen just stared out the window at the spacious pasture, where Emmett's great Belgians grazed on the sparse December grass now graced with a light comforter of snow. She thought of the horse and carriage waiting patiently for her and her husband, Sylvester, just past the front door. The sleek Arabian stallion, whose fine coat mocked the impending northern winter, was Sylvester's pride and joy.

Mattie broke Helen's train of thought as she bustled over and said, "Well, let's go see what the world crisis is now!" Mattie marched out of the room with Helen in tow and faced the sitting room, hands firmly planted on her abundant hips. "Now, just what are you two fellows carrying on about? Can't you give your poor wives a chance to have a nice chat—ever? Why, at your ages, you should be ashamed of yourselves!"

"Goodness, yes," Helen murmured bravely from the safety of Mattie's rear quarter. Emmett glared past the plate of warm, but untouched, apple fritters on the table, to the window where Sylvester was studying the deep fall afternoon in stubborn silence. The clock's ticking was like a countdown, and the silence was soon broken by Emmett.

"The old coot just won't admit a plain fact of life in these parts!" he started. "Which," he continued, "simply stated for our *foreign* friends, is that a man should have at least *one* decent horse in his lifetime. Or at least admit when he don't!" Sylvester turned his slim body with a taunting grin. "Well, my sod-busting friend, at least when I take my Helen into town *my* rig doesn't thunder and shake the gas lamps off the parson's house! No! I am blessed with admiring glances and the pleasure of a spirited and sensitive animal to which I trust my most precious possession." With that, he turned to look at Helen, whose slight form was nearly obliterated to sight by Mattie's plump, wholesome body.

"Shake the gas lamps?" Emmett exploded. "Shake! Why, the only thing shaking around here are those pods rolling around in your bean-sprout brain! That, and that useless white bag of bones out there!"

With that, Emmett snatched his hat from the sofa, Helen hurried to grab her bag, and Mattie rushed back to the kitchen to package a few homemade pies and canned fruits for her sister to take home. Helen followed Mattie to the kitchen, and they paused to hug and say good-bye. Mattie said, "I never even had a chance to ask how the store is doing—is all well in town?" Helen replied, "Oh, things are going fine. I just wish things were better with the men. "

She accentuated her comment with a head toss to the parlor and then with a brief pat on Mattie's shoulder as she turned to join Sylvester, who had the spirited gray horse and fancy carriage turned toward the road. "Bye, Emmett," Helen called, and Emmett responded with a grunt. The rhythmic clip-clop of the horse's hooves faded into the distance. Mattie picked up the dishes and stuck out her tongue at Emmett's huge frame as he lumbered past her and out of the house. *Stubborn old farmer,* she thought, *Crotchety old storekeeper! A horse is a horse! Lordy me, what shall we do?*

This war had begun years and years ago, when Sylvester had come into the sleepy German community in central Wisconsin on business and proceeded to woo and sweep Mattie's pretty young sister, Helen, off her feet. Emmett and Mattie farmed nearly one hundred acres on good, tillable ground—and when it became apparent that Helen was in love, Mattie became terribly worried that her only sister would marry and leave the small farming community, and the house next store that their folks had left them, for Sylvester's polished and exciting world. With much cajoling, and because the small general store in the nearby town of Buck Creek was up for sale, Helen was able to persuade Sylvester to stay, with the promise that they would run the small business together. Stay he did, and they married. One day, amid great excitement at the railroad station, a crowd of passersby gathered as a frightened, wide-eyed gray stallion leapt off the ramp of the boxcar.

Hooves flashed in the sun and skidded sharply as the horse was led from the train and through the respectfully parted crowd. "What's 'e gonna do w'im?" mused one farmer to another, whose only response was a thoughtful scratching of his beard.

At home, Sylvester proudly showed Helen his special gift. The horse, whose slick coat had dried from the nervous sweat, focused with keen curiosity on Helen and his unfamiliar surroundings. He appeared to begin to accept his new home with a cubed apple fed from Helen's small hand. "He's just—why, he's just—different!" she exclaimed. "And so—so—so beautiful!"

"So proud!" Sylvester boomed. "A purebred Arabian from fine descendants! The most intelligent creature on earth." He added, "The mares are coming! We'll have a barn full of the most dazzling animals in this wretched state!" At Helen's shocked look, he quickly said, "Of course, what I mean is that this horse, dear Helen, will be a most fitting animal for a man to drive the prettiest girl in town about with."

Helen smiled, but she wondered doubtfully, as most people in town did, what the horse was good for. After all, the big, golden Belgians, the dappled Percherons, and the mighty Shire workhorses could pull the plows, bring in the hay and crops, and drive groceries and supplies from town. They could clear rock-strewn fields for new cropland, harvest the corn and wheat, and pull the family wagon to church and festivals. Why, they even helped raise barns with their strong, supple muscles and powerful backs, and they were kind, quiet servants to the hardworking people who owned them. "Sylvester, he's just wonderful," Helen said as she smiled weakly and turned to go.

"Wait! Just wait until we pull into town tomorrow! Why, he'll knock 'em dead!" Sylvester exclaimed as he rubbed the horse's silky nose. He left then to try out the beautiful patent leather harness and elegant trappings on his newly acquired prize.

A few weeks later, Sylvester surprised the community again by shipping in via railcar three purebred Arabian mares. Emmett and the other farmers sniffed and snorted at the sight of Sylvester's small band, and it gave them constant entertainment during get-togethers to think up an assortment of names for Sylvester's horses, none of them nice. When Sylvester would drive by Emmett's place, the big workhorses would thunder to the fence at the road and stare with unabashed delight at the fine Arabians trotting smartly along, towing the top-hatted Sylvester in his prim carriage. Sylvester took great pride in driving his fine gray to and from the little general store, and especially peacocked about on Sundays for the ride to church, when the elegant Arab clearly outshone his burly equine counterparts. His big workhorse brethren stood stoically alongside the delicate, big-eyed Arab, who shook his fine mane and played incessantly with his bit while impatiently awaiting the final "Amen."

When services were over, Sylvester never lost the opportunity to chat with the parson for a few moments, giving Emmett a head start, so that, when he did leave, Sylvester could trot briskly past Emmett and Mattie in their lumbering wagon in front of the townsfolk. Sylvester would wave gaily to Emmett with a tip of his brim and would then speed on by to the clatter of steel-shod hooves and more than a little dust. Mattie would shade her eyes, and Emmett would swear. "The Lord's Day!" Mattie would exclaim, "Control yourself!"

At other times, Sylvester would brag of his horse's abilities, intelligence and endurance. Emmett would counter by reminding Sylvester that Rome wasn't built by midgets, fields didn't get plowed by schoolgirls, and no horse worth his salt had a head the size of a teacup! The feud continued for years.

One Saturday in mid-December, both men set out on a blustery, sleet-soaked morning for tasks that would take them down the heavily wooded road to Buck Creek. Sylvester was going to town to arrange delivery of a large order for his shop; he would meet the 2:00 train. Emmett, on the other hand, did his chores until mid-morning, when he embarked on a special journey, ax in hand. He planned to chop down a most spectacular little Christmas tree for Mattie, which he had seen growing just off the main road on the way to Buck Creek. As Sylvester was leaving for town, Emmett was returning from his task, with the snow-covered pine bouncing fragrantly in the back of his wagon, along with one that Mattie had insisted he chop down for Helen—a short, misshapen one that he had hewn with reckless glee. A short time later, his big Belgian perked up his ears and nickered. Just around the next curve, Emmett discovered Sylvester, with his horse and carriage at a dead stop. Emmett pulled up with a long, "Whoa, boy," as they all stared at the huge tree that had fallen and blocked the road. Emmett glared at Sylvester. "And I suppose you put this here just to spite me!"

Sylvester returned the comment by rearranging his woolen muffler and furred lap-jacket. "No—oh goodness, no, brother—I'd have had it wait just a moment longer with hopes that you'd be beneath it!"

The men glared at the tree. Sylvester sniffed, "I really have to make that train—it would be ten miles back and around on a lesser road."

Emmett conceded, his mouth watering at the thought of Mattie's homemade bread cooling on the oven rack above the simmering luncheon roast. He replied, "I'm sure the thought occurred to you that it is just as far out of *my* way!"

Sylvester sighed. "Yes, I did, unless … unless …" The solution was evident, but neither brother-in-law cared to admit it. If Emmett took Sylvester's buggy home, and Sylvester took Emmett's buggy to town, they could both get their day's work done. Finally, two brakes creaked, and Sylvester's finely crafted overshoes hit the hard ground as Emmett's workboots did. The switch was on.

They walked toward one another and clambered over the tree. From the other side, Sylvester turned to Emmett and said, "Go easy on his mouth! He's very sensitive!" and then under his breath, spat, *you big brute!*

Emmett fired back, "It's about time you drove a real one, anyway!" Then, with a groan of springs, his massive frame filled the whole driver's seat of Sylvester's carriage. Sylvester felt bewildered behind the large singletree and the Belgian's huge rump as he awkwardly gathered the thick leather reins and clumsily turned the big wagon around. A few moments later they were gone from each other's sight.

Hours later, Sylvester's horse was rubbed down and fed, and the carriage stood drying off in the barn's wide aisle, while Emmett rested contentedly after his plentiful supper. Mattie was bustling about, getting ready for the trip to Helen's house. Mattie had convinced Emmett to take her for a rare trip—as long as an exchange had to be made on the vehicles, why not make the best of it? They bundled up for the trip, and as Emmett helped Mattie into the fancy black carriage, he paused to stare at the elegant gray horse awaiting their departure. "Whatever are you thinking?" Mattie asked suspiciously.

"Nothing," Emmett replied, but it wasn't true. He was thinking of how much darn fun he'd had driving the trim black rig back to the house. The horse was hugely responsive, yet mannerly. The brisk energy and animation of the Arabian was only topped by his sensitivity to the driver's commands and his desire to please. Emmett had felt years peel off as the fresh cold air met his face, and he'd had to resist the urge to put the horse through a free gallop in the stretch that he'd raced his father's horses through as a youngster. The drive to Sylvester's house was made even more remarkable when Emmett's hand reached for Mattie's beneath the furred horsehair cape. Mattie could only blush and steal a surprised peek at Emmett, who glanced back with a juvenile grin. *Whatever has gotten into him?* she wondered as she warmly tightened her grip on Emmett's.

In the meantime, Sylvester had finished his chore in town

and was heading back on the alternative route, which was lesser traveled and rough. The buckboard creaked as a heavy snow began to fall. Sylvester's hands became numb, and his grip loosened on the reins, but the Belgian walked sturdily on, oblivious to the conditions and the rutted road. Sylvester found himself nearly dozing off as he bounced along in that winter wonderland, what with the peaceful snow falling all about and his work complete. All of a sudden, he was jolted to reality by the steep decline and obvious deterioration of the crude road, which was leading up to a nasty water crossing full of downed limbs and rock. In a panic, he hit the bottom and steered the horse with all of his strength to the right. The obedient horse complied, and with that, a large rock lodged between the wheels, and the wagon came to a jack-knifed halt as Sylvester shouted, "Whoa!" Sylvester was propelled off the seat and into the rocky bed below. His head hit a large boulder, and he was instantly knocked unconscious. He landed between the heavily shirred fetlocks of the horse's plate-sized feet and the front wheel. If the horse moved, he would surely be killed.

Back at Helen and Sylvester's house, Mattie and Helen were joyfully reacquainted as Emmett unhitched the horse and brushed him to a gleam. He put up the horse and settled in to wait for Sylvester and his wagon to arrive. When the girls were finally talked out some time later, the skies were dark. Although the sisters marveled at the length and uninterrupted gaiety of their visit, they were getting deeply worried about Sylvester. Emmett put their minds at ease by telling them that Sylvester was quite safe, and that he could come to no harm behind the reins of Emmett's most trusted gelding. "That horse knows his way home," he said. "And he'll get him here—I'd stake my place on it." However, he too was concerned, as it was far past the time that Sylvester should have been back.

During this time, Sylvester passed in and out of consciousness in the stream bed. The staunch gelding stood stock-still as he had been instructed, remembering well his training and the many hours of field work under Emmett's firm command. Although his legs were ice encrusted, and the snow no longer melted on his wide back, the big horse stood quietly in ankle-deep water awaiting his master's voice. Sylvester weakly awakened and struggled to right himself in the frigid creek. He was able to gain his senses and, with sheer determination, lift himself up and into the wagon where he gathered the reins and hollered, "Hup!" to the mighty steed. With that, he wrapped the reins about his hands and slumped backward into the soft pine bed behind the seat. The horse lurched forward and dug in. He managed to loosen the wagon from its lodging in the stubborn rock and, with steady gait, he pulled the buckboard up the steep hill and headed for home.

> When horse and wagon arrived at Emmett's farm, Emmett was already there. Helen had become frantic, nearing hysteria, and Emmett had promised to go and find the missing Sylvester. He was just heading out when he heard the familiar ringing and jostling of his rig and looked on in amazement as the great Belgian lumbered up the drive and stopped, driverless. Emmett ran to the wagon and peered over the side to see Sylvester, crumpled and cold. When he saw the watery blood on Sylvester's white muffler, he acted quickly, gathering the man up as if he were a child and shuffling him inside to warmth, dry clothing, and a glass of brandy. Sylvester slowly came around, and when he did, he rose unsteadily to shake Emmett's hand. "Your horse saved my life," he said. "I would have been dead with a lesser beast."

Emmett acknowledged this with a firm grip and bit his lip. "Yours ain't so bad, either," he said, and they gave each other wry smiles.

Two weeks later, Mattie and Helen were once again sipping coffee in Mattie's spacious kitchen, on a gorgeous Christmas morning. "Can you believe it?" Helen said, still in awe of the miracle that had occurred. "I wouldn't have thought this day would come in a million years! Those two exchanging *gifts!*"

Mattie laughed. Their laughter was disturbed by an increasingly loud discussion taking place in the parlor. "Uh-oh," Mattie said with a frown, and they went into the parlor to find Emmett and Sylvester once again engaged in a heated exchange of words—in front of a little crooked pine tree. Upon learning of Emmett's indiscretion, Mattie had put her foot down in a most imposing way and the perfect pine tree that he had chopped down for Mattie had been hastily exchanged for the other. However, it was gaily adorned with handmade decorations and a colorful string of cranberries, and it was here that Sylvester stood gracefully as he tipped his glass to Emmett, who was plopped on the couch.

"The mighty Emmett and I," he began, "were simply *discussing* the merit of training the horse to the cart."

Emmett glanced up at the women and replied, "Now, if you don't mind, we'd like to be left alone!"

Mattie and Helen looked at one another quizzically and then retreated to the warm kitchen, to the good-natured laughter of the men. "Don't argue with it, dear," Mattie said as she basted the turkey. "This is the best Christmas yet!" Helen just beamed.

Meanwhile, out in Emmett's barn, the yearling Arabian nuzzled the kind, whiskered nose of the Belgian mare in the tie stall next to him before he returned to his Christmas feast of Emmett's alfalfa, Mattie's mash, and a treat of carrots sprinkled with sugar. In Sylvester's barn, the creamy Belgian filly dwarfed her petite Arabian stallmate, but she patiently tolerated the spirited playfulness of the youngster as she took in her new, fancy home. The late December sun filtered gently through the frosty window, and the ice began to melt in that small community of Buck Creek.

Anything's Possible . . .

The tale of a grizzled old curmudgeon, a handsome young man, and a big bay horse. Slip on some boots and take a ride!

Just below the foothills of the South Range, and due north of where it fed into the tumbling body of the big mountains, an old man sat alone on his one good wooden porch step, all smooth and polished by the years and the boots and the denim. He stared down at his bum leg, and he then reached behind him for the Skoal can and grumbled at its sparse contents. "Man can't make a damned livin' and can't enjoy the lousy livin' he makes," he muttered as he pinched out a meager supply of the tobacco. Past the crook in his driveway, a motion caught his eye that wasn't looking like a horse or a cow a'tall. Wil stood up on his decent leg and shaded his eyes, squinting at the figure approaching the house. The dust from the stranger's feet made a low, reddish cloud that refused to dispel in the airless early evening. As the sun was on his back, the man's features and face were as vague as the dust itself.

Wil waited long enough and then his surly temper and suspicious nature took over. "And just who in Sam Hill are you?" he snorted, smacking his cane tip on the hollow step to accentuate his demand.

"Hey, Boss, relax," returned the man, who was now slowing his pace to stop. He set down the duffel bag he had slung over his back and said, "I'm here to give you a hand—I need some work, and I was told by Curly in town to come up here and see you. Said you might hire me. I don't want much in the way of money, but I do like to stay dry, and from the looks of your roof," he continued, peering above the old man, "that might be tough."

Wil glared at the young man and his brashness, and then he spat on the ground to emphasize his next few words. "Tough, ya say?" he growled, "I'll tell ya what's tough, you young, dumb buck! It's tough walking clear on back down to that no-good barbershop in town this time of day and giving old Curly a message from the Raven H Ranch! And this, my friend," Wil sputtered, waving his arm around behind him, "is the Taj Mahal compared to the bunkhouse 'round back where the likes of you'd be setting yer bedroll!"

The young fellow could clearly see that Wil was blowing up a good head of steam, so he bowed slightly to acknowledge the older man's authority and stuck his hand out. "My name's Jim. I do like your place, and I do need the job. "

Wil looked down at Jim's hand in disgust. He cocked his head like a banty rooster. "Why, them rosy-soft paws of your'n couldn't do me a day's good. You wouldn't last a week! Go on, get on out of here!"

Like a pair of tomcats, Wil and Jim stared deep into one another's eyes, until Wil finally broke and sat back down heavily on the stair. "Doggone leg," he mumbled. Jim picked up his heavy bag and took a step backward, and then another. Wil said nothing as he watched Jim depart. Finally he swore and hollered out, "Hey, the bunks are out back, you sorry son of a gun. And I don't pay for no lollygaggin' or whiskey. Be back out here in ten minutes, and we'll see how much work is in you!"

Jim stopped and turned his head, taking it all in: the forlorn, sagging little house, the missing posts on the corral, the slight lean to the shed where yellowed wisps of old hay were poking through the tired siding. He saw a herd of horses behind a big, shaggy barn; their broad, dark backs were visible in the distance. An overgrown heifer of undetermined breeding bellowed her presence from the vicinity of a round pen, and a small, lame mare hobbled around loose in the yard, pausing here and there to pick at some weedy excuse for grass poking through the rock-hard ground.

Jim nodded his head and smiled to himself. "Perfect!" he thought as he tipped his cap to Wil and nosed his way around back. He entered the small bunkhouse, which was no more than a lean-to on the back of the house. He looked around at its bare contents. Two army-style cots and an old pedestal table were the main furnishings, and a faded calendar dated 1951 boasted the pin-up beauties of the day. Fresh-looking ladies with rouged cheeks and wearing frilly little rompers stared back at him with gay eyes and friendly smiles—their big straight teeth were now yellowed with age. "Afternoon, ladies," Jim said. He threw his roll on the cot, whose springs groaned their surprise. A grimy glass-covered photo caught his eye, and he rubbed the dust off to reveal a picture of a seal-brown horse—a stallion, it seemed, whose big hazel eyes and intelligent expression drew Jim closer. The man whistled when he read the name: "Thunder Bay. Owned by Wil Raven." Thunder Bay had been one of the greats—pure foundation quarter horse and the best all-around horse of his time. "The old man has a bit of history here," mused Jim as he readied himself to go outside. With another look around, he said, "Just wonder what happened."

Wil was still sitting on the porch when Jim came around the house to talk to him. They began to discuss Jim's duties, and Wil's first question took the other man by surprise. "Can ya sew?" he queried.

Jim stared at the old guy and replied, "No, I don't sew, and I don't cook, and I don't do wash. I don't wear a skirt, and I never made a bed in my life. I'm a decent shot with a revolver, and I play a damned good game of tennis and a fair game of poker. I ride a horse as good as the next, maybe better, but I don't back down, and I sure as hell don't sew. Or milk cows," he ended, with a short glance to the heifer.

Wil thought to himself, *Well, what in the devil* are *ya good for?* Instead, he said, "I got some harness needs sewing, and the canvas over my hay needs repairin'. I got plenty of saddles needing oil, and horses to work, and a few places in the fence to mend. You hold a hammer as good as that revolver?"

Jim set one lean leg on the stoop and stuck his hand out one more time. "First things first," he said, and as Wil returned the handshake, Jim grinned. Old and young gripped one another with some degree of understanding, setting off on perhaps the biggest task of all—stretching a fence made of time itself.

The next day proved interesting enough, as Jim began sorting things out on the ranch—after a well-cooked and welcome breakfast, compliments of Wil. The old man hobbled around behind Jim, pointing out the various hidey-holes for the tools and tack and giving pointed advice all along the way, which Jim weakly acknowledged. *Thinks he knows it all*, they both thought to themselves. The lame mare, comically, followed the pair around the ranch, and once Jim turned to suppress a laugh as Wil's seriousness was well eroded by a very large and very long yawn from the horse at his shoulder.

As the first week went by, nails were pounded and some new poles set. As Wil watched from his well-worn perch on the stair, he was lulled to sleepiness by the steady *thud-puff*, *thud-puff* of the tamping tool. The clay and the sweat turned Jim's ball cap into a nondescript lid that summed up the day's work. "How's those hands?" Wil hollered on the third day.

Jim hesitated and looked down to see the blisters, the raw, red spots, and the brand-new calluses beginning to sprout in their place. "Just fine!" he replied cheerfully as he clapped them together and gave Wil the old thumbs-up with one. The next day, a pair of old, but oiled, leather gloves hung on the bunkhouse door, and Jim gratefully slipped them on.

Two weeks went by, and as they were eating dinner one evening, Jim asked about the horses. "When do we get around to riding?" he said, glancing up.

"Well," Wil said slowly, "I guess there might be some time after dinner this week. Let's take the truck now and go on out there, and I'll point out a few that you can start on. " They finished up, cleared the table, and then headed out the rutted path to the horses, whose heads poked up like so many wild deer in a valley. The horses stared at truck and humans with interest. The herd was comprised of five or six mares and a husky brown horse that Jim recognized to be a stallion, while further down grazed three or four youngsters.

"We'll start with the yellow filly," declared Wil from his seat on the truck.

Jim, excited about the prospects of riding, leaned out to get a better look. "You mean the little one right there to the left of the mouse colored horse?"

"Yep," replied Wil. "She's the one." They circled the horses once more, and Jim turned the truck around with some feeling of disappointment. There was a nice big bay mare out there that looked like a good mover, but the little palomino was small and plain—not much to look at and less to get enthused about.

They caught the little palomino up the next afternoon. Jim's weariness disappeared as he thought about his next and most illustrious chore. "She broke at all?" Jim queried as he pulled saddle and blanket from the tack room. This was now pretty much de-cobwebbed, and what had been a tangled mess of harness was now hung neatly on the wall.

"Well, sure, she's broke," Wil spat, "Rode her myself up until my leg got buggered up. Was breaking her for a friend up the road. Cow horse. "

"You got a snaffle bit out here, Wil? I don't see one," Jim asked.

"Got lots of bits and bridles there. Use this one," Wil replied as he pulled out an old, discolored-looking thing from the rack. Jim examined it and decided it was made for a plow horse or a circus horse but not a riding horse. "Think I'll take the bosal," he said, and with that he took saddle and bosal to the corral where the young mare awaited them.

Wil sat down on a stump and watched as Jim approached the mare. She blew softly at the man, but it was more out of curiosity than fear. Jim quietly placed the headgear on the mare and called to Wil. "Got a brush?"

"What for?" Wil responded.

Jim turned back to the mare and used the flat of his hand to check her back and girth area for dirt and burrs, and after finding her relatively clean, he eased blanket and saddle up over her back and slowly tightened the girth. Jim walked her a step or two and then rechecked the girth, tightening it to his satisfaction, and then he lowered the stirrups. The mare responded calmly as he gathered up the thick, soft reins and stepped lightly to her back. As they walked off, he thought of how strange the smooth leather saddle felt to his jeans—not a bad-feeling saddle, but certainly not the gear he was accustomed to. The mare walked around the corral several times, until Jim asked her for a trot, which she picked up smoothly and evenly. "She's better gaited than I thought," Jim said loudly in the direction of the tree stump. As he jogged the horse into circles, he was impressed with her willingness and ears-up attitude. He rode the mare for a pretty good while, hoping that Wil was picking up on how light his hands were and how even his profile was, even grinning to himself, for he knew he'd made a striking duo with nearly any horse he'd ever sat upon.

Jim decided to lope the mare, and as he asked her, he watched her trim little ears go flat back. She exploded in a fit and dumped Jim like a sack of mortar mix on the hard clay floor of the arena. She quit her pitching about the time Jim staggered to his feet, knocking the dust off his jeans and sputtering all the swear words that felt the best. Smoke curled up from the pipe in Wil's hand as he watched without a word. Jim snugged his hat back on and walked up to the mare. Without a moment's hesitation, he was back up on her, jogging her around and doing his best to suppress his anger at himself for letting the mare fly off the handle while he had sat there unprepared. This time, he gathered up his reins real tight and laid back in the saddle a bit, waiting for her to blow up when he asked once again for the lope. What the yellow filly did was to yank the reins out ahead of Jim in a well-practiced move that unsettled him, and while he managed the first wild jump, the second loosened him up a notch, and the third jump sent Jim sailing.

Jim jumped back up and grabbed the thick reins as the filly stood waiting for him, her prim little ears flicking and her watchful eyes regarding him with what must certainly have been a bit of horse humor. "Third time's the ticket," Jim muttered to himself as he heaved himself up once again. Most of his equitation finesse and ego had been left down in the dirt. Jim wore the filly down with some long trotting and circling, and when she was blowing pretty good, he gigged her firmly and held those reins with all the strength he had, waiting for the first plunge. The ears went down, and the mare pulled hard once, and then stuck her nose through the bosal. Like a runaway cart horse, she took off with great, leaping dives across the corral, not really bucking, but getting herself into position should she decide to really explode. Jim sat up cleanly in the saddle, but he knew, as the mare did, that he had not the slightest bit of control. He used both of his hands in a last-ditch effort to slow her and pulled her head around to the right as hard as he could, until she came to a heaving stop right in front of the old man. They looked at one another for a moment, and before Wil could utter a word, Jim said, "I'll just take that now," pointing to the bridle with the old browned bit that Wil had been sitting on. Things progressed a bit better from there on, but, just the same, Jim decided the lope could wait for another day or so.

Another day, Jim was up on the hay shed, arranging the newly repaired canvas over its sides, when he paused, as he did often, to look out at the big bay stallion that Wil owned. The horse was a six-year-old son of the best breeding stallion produced by old Thunder Bay, out of a world-class mare who had swept the Denver Stock Show some years back in every event she'd been entered in. He was halter broke and little else, but his near-perfect conformation and keen head caused Jim to feel an excitement about the horse that he'd never felt before. He longed to work with the animal and to feel his strong back beneath his seat; a horse of such magnificent proportion was a temptation that Jim found very difficult to resist. He pestered Wil constantly to let him start the stallion and to get him broke to saddle, for, in the back of his mind, Jim knew that he had to one day own him. Wil kept putting Jim off, never really saying why, but with a ferocity that Jim knew he shouldn't cross. Jim went back to his duties on the roof, but he was determined to change Wil's mind.

It was now late in July. One day, after the riding chores were finished on a few of Wil's colts, Jim went and knocked on the door of the ranch house and let himself in. The red glow of the sunset flooded in behind him. He sat himself down at the battered kitchen table where Wil was fooling around with his old wristwatch that had stopped running. "Think I might stroll into town tomorrow," Jim said. "I sure could use a shave and a haircut and a few things from the general store."

Wil just kept fussing with the old watch, and, after a few moments of silence, he arose and took two jelly glasses from the cabinet, along with a bottle of bourbon, and placed them on the table. "If you're going to see old Curly," he said slowly, "you're gonna need some of this. Before *and* after!" Jim grinned and toasted the old man when his glass was poured. "Here's to old Curly. And to Thunder Bay." Wil took a good sip and rolled his glass around in his hand, staring into its mellow contents and reflecting upon heaven only knew what.

"Yep, Thunder Bay ... he was a good'un," Wil said. "Best damned horse I ever set on, and not only that! The best durn producin' stallion a man could get his hands on. And for a long time, at that. Paid for my first car with 'im, got me my first wife with 'im, coulda silverplated this whole room with 'im!" Wil went on and on, talking about the horse and the good times as if it had been yesterday. Jim listened and laughed at Wil's stories as they unraveled in pieces and bits. They were bittersweet recollections of pride and hard-won successes, dosed with discouragement at times; they were embellished by the years and the telling. Wil's eyes sparkled as he told of the horse's triumphs, and they glistened, at the end, when he spoke of the old stallion's death. There was a long silence when Wil finished as the two men sat and looked into the woodstove's flames licking away at the logs.

"Well, I know it's not crazy to think that the bay out there couldn't be good, maybe even as good as the old boy himself," Jim exclaimed. "He's got the looks, he's got the moves, he's got it all! I could take him to the top, Wil, and make him a new champion. I could do it, Wil; I really could do it—he's got everything it takes!"

"That he don't, son," Wil replied. "He has no papers. " Wil sighed and went on to explain that his ex-wife held the paperwork on the last crop of Thunder Bay's foals, and "she'd a dropped dead before she'd a given me any one of 'em. As it is, I don't know where she'd be now, and believe me, you or the man upstairs ain't about to change her mind anyway. I've tried, kid. "

Jim took stock of the new information and stretched out his long legs on the hardwood floor. "Anything's possible in the big city, Wil," he said. "Anything." Jim looked up in earnest and said, "Let me have him to break—my way—will you do that?"

Wil nodded. "Have at him, boy. I might just enjoy the show. "

"And one more thing," Jim added. "I've kinda figgered out a name for him." He paused for a moment and said hopefully, "Boston Bay. Call him Boss for short. One for you in there, one for me, and one for his grandpappy. "

Wil thought about that puzzle for a bit and then assented. "Boston Bay it is," he conceded.

Dawn hadn't yet properly broken the next day as Jim pulled on his jeans and slipped the lariat from its hook on the door of his room. He started up the truck and banged on Wil's door. He heard the old man cussing from within. "Need your help!" Jim shouted and backed off as the door swung wide. "We're gonna rope us a horse—and you're doing the roping! So get those god-awful long johns covered up, and get on out here!" Wil shook out his tangled mop and disappeared, grousing, and soon they were on their way across the bumpy pasture in the early light, heading for the herd.

Wil shook out a loop and swung the rope slowly and deliberately in the direction of the bay stallion. "Give him lots of rope and be mighty careful here," he warned Jim, who was ready to take the helm at the drop of the lariat. The lariat snugged down over the stallion's deep neck, and Jim braced for the pull as the horse drew up in surprise. Boston Bay stood stock-still for a split second and then took a few hesitant steps in the direction of the men. At the tug of the rope, he walked right on up and stood obediently before Jim, who curled the rope cautiously and faced the horse not two feet away with wariness. "Didn't I tell ya he was halter broke?" Wil said calmly as he stepped back into the truck. He drove off, grinning ear to ear. "Follow ya like a dog!" he shouted as he drove off, and Jim followed, towing Boss, who walked quietly beside him. He reminded himself not to double guess old Wil again.

Boston Bay's training was not a disappointment. Wil watched steadily and without offering advice as Jim began his groundwork, which culminated in some fancy driving assisted by a shiny new snaffle bit purchased in town. Tools and toil were waylaid as Jim spent every available moment with the stud. From sacking to bitting to saddling, the Boss took it all in stride, and by the time Jim lifted his leg onto the saddle, the horse was shaping up into a perceptive animal, tuned not only to his own incredible balance but also to Jim's light touch on the reins. His training progressed from round pen to arena and from arena to flat, open ground, where the two would wander and roam the juniper-covered land with tireless curiosity. Mile-covering jogs lasted long after sunlight in the cool evening air as man and horse meshed thoughts and exchanged signals known only to themselves. Never before had Jim felt this kind of satisfaction; never again would he be satisfied without it. He gloried not in show-ring applause but in the simple joy of riding the green-broke Boston Bay.

Days turned into weeks, and the brown horse progressed. Jim tackled his chores, and rode Wil's young horses, and spent his every wage dollar on new equipment for horses and tools to help him in his jobs. "You never did get that haircut," Wil said one day. "Yer looking mighty rough, son. Take the day in town—take the horse, if you'd like; show 'em what a good one looks like down there!"

Jim grinned and said, "Well, I might just do that. See you later." Soon he had saddled up and ridden off. When he was perhaps two miles from the ranch, he reined the Boss in, the better to see the horizon. He had spotted a car from a mile away, and he immediately recognized its sleek exterior as it churned the red dirt into a snarling cloud of dust behind it. He stopped the horse to watch its weaving approach as the driver steered through swales and holes in the road toward him and Boss. When Jim could see through the gritted pane the man at the wheel, he calmly stepped Boss into the path of the vehicle, causing the car to swerve badly and slide to a rest amid the dust, and the pebbles, and the clear, quiet valley air.

The response was quick. The darkened pane of the window rolled silently down, and the man at the wheel stared with pistol-point eyes at Jim. The exchange was brief. "I'm looking for Wil Raven's place," the man spouted. "And a young man named Jim. I don't suppose you'd tell me where to find the place?" Jim pictured himself in his mind: the grizzled beard and thick hair crowding his frayed collar in shards, the colorless jeans, and the rolled-up sleeves exposing muscular arms tanned and toughened by the sun and the sweat. He said nothing as he watched his father's stern frown from behind the door of the elegant Porsche. He was teasing the other man's patience and reveling in the knowledge. "Well? Do you know or don't you?" said his father impatiently.

"Do you know or don't you?" Jim replied solidly. Father looked at son with a lost expression as he rebounded from his surprise and swung the door wide to better see the young man on the horse.

"Just what the devil do you think you're doing?" his father exploded, his voice rising as he went on. "I send you to the finest equestrian camp in the Southwest, and I find out you're not there—never even showed—do you have *any* idea of what I have been through the last few weeks looking for you? *Do you?*"

The silence was strained as Jim contemplated his answer, the thoughts turning over in his mind as they had for the last month or so. He savored the moment as it bathed over the pain and the hurt that he'd felt over the years of growing up without the love and nourishment of his parents. They had always been too busy—too busy to see his high-school graduation, too consumed in their own affairs to watch their son carry the winning cup off the field, too careless to notice the stoic, empty victories and sorry-sweet conquests of his childhood. Jim flatly stated, "I'm not going back, Dad."

His father gripped the top edge of the car door and fisted the other. "Your semester is paid up, Jim. School started last week—you promised me, dang it all—you promised me you'd get your education, and we agreed on it! What's happened to you, I don't know. This is a complete embarrassment for your mother and me. " He looked off to the rising mountain ledges in the distance and then back. "But I do know this—you're coming back to Boston. Now. "

Jim looked down at the scuffed-up saddle horn and the soft, dark mane of Boss gently whisking by his fingers in the low breeze. "No, Dad. No, I'm not. "

"We'll see about that," said his father. The conversation was over, as far as the elder man was concerned, and with a last, searing look, he turned the car around and drove off in a spew of gravel and rocks that startled the horse. As Jim settled him, he watched the disappearing bumper with cool detachment and a satisfaction that reached deeper than old Wil's rusted well.

Four days later, the big silver-winged jet crowned the snow-covered peaks

121

in the purple air over the New Mexican border. Jim drew a deep breath and closed his eyes to all beyond the window to his right. Going home was the toughest part of it all. After his ride that day, Jim had had a long talk with Wil. He'd exposed his life like a journey into a faraway land, ending with the abrupt meeting in the roadway. Wil had had little to say, and when he did speak, he'd spoken with plain old wisdom and feelings that were a whole lot easier thought than said.

"If I'd a given you a job, Jim, and you hadn't finished it, I'd a been pretty disappointed in you. As it is, I've given you lots of jobs, and you've done every one to the best of what you know. Now, I'm not sayin' they was the prettiest jobs I ever seen," he said, glancing over for Jim's benefit at the slightly crooked siding that Jim had installed, "but you did 'em. I think you oughta finish this job of schoolin', if that's what you started. "

Jim looked down at his boots and replied, "Can I stay on?"

Wil got up to end the conversation. "You do what's right, boy. You do what you have to do. "

Jim's thoughts tumbled and turned as he struggled to accept his decision to return to Boston on that moody flight. His heart was as cold as the eastern sky when night fell in the heavens, the night that would take him back to a life that bore him along as if in a rudderless raft. Already he missed Wil, and the ranch, and the smell of hardwood chips smoking in the ancient stove this time of day. He could hear Boston Bay calling his mares and see the little crippled mare lazing beneath the scarred tree in the yard as the sun pushed a rim of red over the edge of the mountains. He dozed off, and when he awoke, the flight had landed.

Time passed, and Wil's leg was better, but the weeks went by slowly, the chores got longer, and the days ended in monotony. He missed Jim more than he cared to admit. Why, at his age, he'd been through it all, but this time it felt different. Doggone it, nothing was the same. As winter set in, the old woodstove didn't even feel as warm, and at the first snowfall, Wil didn't feel the urge to walk out the door and watch its pretty descent, as was his habit. He didn't feel like riding, and he didn't feel like fixing things. About all he did care to do was go into town and sit for hours at the little café, staring at the other old cranks who came in to play checkers or solve the world's problems. There wasn't much mail, and as he sat there, he watched the cardboard Thanksgiving turkeys on the café window come down and the cardboard Christmas trees go up. The stack of newspapers grew in the corner to measure the days and weeks. The UPS man arrived at noontime nearly every other day to deliver the growing number of packages, which was pretty exciting, considering the fact that he was the only fresh face in town. He sported a ponytail and wore a gold chain necklace, which prompted much speculation and idle talk amongst the oldsters.

One day, the UPS man had a small package for Wil. Wil held it in his hands, shook his head, and then tossed it distractedly behind the seat of his pickup truck. He wrote out two Christmas cards: one to his brother in Oklahoma and one to Jim, but no answering card came forth in the days before Christmas. Christmas Eve arrived with a surly northwest wind to match Wil's temper. He sat in his usual chair at the café, watching his friends and neighbors exchange pleasantries and news, not really feeling up to all that backslapping and hand-shaking and general good holiday cheer that made his head go to hurting. He finished his meal and watched out the window as the big brown truck came rumbling into town once again. He muttered a few words to himself about "all that good money goin' to waste on department-store gifts when most folks couldn't afford a decent pair of pants around town." The truck rolled to a stop in front of the café and out stepped the driver and his lone passenger.

The sight of Jim startled Wil so badly that he nearly fell off the chair he was perched on in his haste to get up and out the door—he remembered his gruff composure just in time as the young man turned to go down the street. "Hey, kid! Hey, what in the devil are you doin' here, when you should be home with your family today?"

Jim turned around and faced Wil, a broad smile lighting up his face. "And what in the devil you doin' out on the street with no jacket on in this lousy wind?" Jim said.

"Get in the truck, son! I'll be right out!" Wil said excitedly as he rushed back in to the restaurant, nearly causing the waitress to drop her tray as he flew by her.

On the ride back to the ranch, the truck was filled with talk, and it seemed to Jim that Wil regarded him as a specter, or a vision, the way the old guy kept looking at him. When they reached the Raven H Ranch, Wil grabbed a few chunks of wood off the pile to warm things inside, and he insisted that Jim bring his bags in—no bunkhouse tonight. Wil just kept shaking his head, so very glad to see his young partner again—sorry to say, the only person he could say he'd missed in a long, long time. They talked about the time between, and the horses, and Jim's schooling, and when Wil asked about the family, Jim told him it was the usual—his parents were away for the holidays. "Me, too, this time," Jim laughed, and he poked Wil in the shoulder. "Mind if I stay for more than one?"

"Well, what do you mean?" asked Wil.

"Schooling can wait, Boss. There's one bay horse out there that I missed even more than you and this shipwreck of a place you call home. We're going to Congress and then to the World Championships, Wil! I just don't want to wait 'til I'm as old and mean as you to get there!" Jim jumped up, dug around in his duffle bag, and pulled out a small package. He handed it to Wil. "Couldn't let Christmas go by without wishing an old friend Merry Christmas, now, could I?"

Wil received the gift and opened it carefully, for it surely didn't weigh much and must be pretty delicate, he felt. An envelope was inside, and as he examined the contents, he sat and stared at the sheet of paper with slackened jaw. When he finally spoke, it was nearly a whisper. "How'd you get these?" he asked as he traced the name of the horse with his finger: "Boston Bay. Registration completed. "

"Anything's possible in the big city, Wil, remember? The Boston Tea Party couldn't hold a candle to my family when it comes to getting what they want. They're real—and they're yours. "

Wil looked to Jim in utter amazement, and then he remembered something. He shuffled out the door to his truck, retrieved the small brown-paper-wrapped package, and gave it to Jim. "Durn near forgot—here, it's for you," he said.

Jim opened the package and whispered, "You knew. You knew I'd be back. "

Inside was a beautiful old sterling-silver bit, inlaid with gold; he could see where the new initials—his own initials—had replaced Wil's, and as he looked at the bit that had once hung in the world-famous Thunder Bay's mouth, he shook his head from side to side. "It's the greatest gift I've ever been given, Wil. Thank you. It'll look just fine when we go to the top. I'll make you proud, Wil, I promise. "

Wil looked at Jim a bit skeptically then. "Yer a long ways from the middle yet. And that silver bit ain't gonna get you there, you know. "

Jim smiled big and began, "Well, anything's possible—"

"Aw, cripes, don't say it!" Wil moaned, and they laughed and grabbed each other in a big bear hug. The fence was stretched—Christmas was embraced—and tomorrow's dreams had begun.

The Gift

"About do it," Dominic said as he boxed up the remaining bolts and auto parts for James, a mechanic by trade. James and Dominic had become fast friends over the years, spending time talking cars, families, and news over Dominic's worn wooden counter in the shop he owned. "How was the funeral, by the way," Dominic asked.

James replied, "Oh, it was good; you know how much Cheri loved her aunt. Getting her started in horses and all."

Dominic smiled. "She still wants another one, huh?"

James stared thoughtfully at the wall of tools and parts and replied, "Yeah. Her aunt left her some money, and it really worries me that she'll get the old bug back and start looking to replace that crazy horse. Man, I sure hope not. "

Dominic nodded in sympathy. "The accident really messed her up. Almost paralyzed … I can see why you wouldn't want to see her go there again. What's it been—five years now?"

"Almost six," James replied. "But her back will never be right. She knows that, too, but every so often she asks about getting some ponies or old rescue horses, or a horse and buggy. Anything to be around horses. I don't even like her donating her time to that horse shelter, but what can I do?" Dominic shook his head in agreement. What could you do about a horse-loving woman?

Cheri was tall, with long, wispy blonde hair and beautiful hazel eyes that viewed the world around her with childlike enchantment. She was like an elegant thoroughbred, lively and energetic, with only a steady, pronounced limp to remind herself that she had survived but had not come out unscathed that day that had forever changed her life. While she was out riding her mare one fresh spring morning, the horse had bolted in fear after a large deer nearly broadsided them, and they had gone end over end through barbed wire and a roadside ditch. The mare had been put down, and the long, painful recovery from her ruined back was made even more difficult for Cheri by the knowledge that she could never ride again.

"Hey, babe!" James called out as Cheri came in the door of their cozy home later that day. They had a nice little farmette on five acres, complete with a mechanics shop, several sheds, and one painfully empty paddock.

"Hi, you!" she replied, and after a quick kiss, they spent some time talking about their day, and then talk turned to what to make for Thanksgiving dinner. The subject became holidays, then Christmas.

"What would my princess like for Christmas this year?" James asked, hoping not to hear yet another plea of an equine nature.

"Well, you know—but I guess I could settle for a new easel," she said with a resigned tone in her voice. Then, brighter, "So what about for you, Mr. Has-It-All?"

James pursed his lips, playfully dragged out the moment, and then said, "Well, that Shelby Mustang would be nice ..."

"Oh really," Cheri laughed, "Don't hold your breath!"

"Well then, what if you just cleaned out that half of the garage for me that has all your old stuff in it——that would be a great gift."

Cheri thought of the carefully cleaned tack, the tack trunk, and her saddles still taking up space for no better reason than the hard-to-let-go memories of her and her lovely mare. "Deal," she said. And with that, they made themselves a little warm fire in the woodstove as the leaves began to twirl about outside in the November breeze.

The weeks flew by, and once again James was leaning on his elbows at Dominic's Garage, shooting the breeze with his good friend. "Saw your wife over at the feed store the other day," said Dominic. "She was looking at the ad board. I kinda snuck up behind her to give her a hug, and she was staring at a photo ad. As in horse and buggy ad. Just thought you might like to know. "

Jim grimaced. His wife had received a pretty sum from her aunt, and there was little he could do but hope that she would not do anything rash—like buy another horse. "I don't hate horses, Dom, I really don't," James said, "but I couldn't handle another scare."

"You may not like horses, James, but, the fact is, she loves them as much as she loves you. I doubt she'd go behind your back; she's not made that way. It's just a shame, that's all."

James drove home slowly, pausing as he usually did in front of the vintage car lot that held the car of his dreams—a Shelby. The 1966 sapphire-blue Mustang GT, gracefully restored with gold racing stripes, sat staring back at him from gleaming headlights as if to say, "Not gonna be here forever, pal—what are you waiting for?" James drove on by and daydreamed about it for about the hundredth time, knowing full well the cost would really rock the boat financially. Still, it was fun to think about it. He pulled into his newly cleaned garage, and his brief feeling of guilt was erased as Cheri, with a welcoming smile, stood at the door to greet him.

Christmas arrived on the blustery north wind, and the day promised to be a cold one, but the Christmas tree was aglow, and as James and Cheri exchanged gifts with one another, they were happily chatting while admiring their presents. Cheri waited until last to open the large package, which held the new art easel. She had become quite the oil painter since her accident, and beautiful horses shone from canvasses throughout the house. "It's wonderful, James—it is! Thank you!"

They heard the doorbell ring, and it was Dominic who greeted them. "Hey, Merry Christmas!" James called out. "What brings you by?"

"Oh, I was just delivering a gift." Because his hands were empty, James gave him a puzzled look and invited him in.

"No, come on outside for a minute." Cheri quickly pulled on a jacket and her boots, and she tugged at James' arm. "Come see!"

With a flourish, Dominic pulled up the garage door—and there within was the Shelby GT. James could only stare at it; he looked to Cheri and then to Dominic. "It's yours, James! It's all yours!" Cheri said with twinkling eyes.

James thought of the inheritance money, and a lump formed in his throat. "But, why? All you wanted—you could have—" he stuttered and then grew silent. He could not complete the sentence.

Cheri glowed. "Because you love it. You love it, and I love you. " With that, Cheri dropped her arms around his neck and kissed her husband, who was still reeling from his gift.

Dominic laughed and said, "You're a lucky man!"

James replied softly, "No, I am a blind one."

Later, on a beautiful spring day, Dominic and James once again stood in James's garage, where the new carriage waited for the perfect horse to pull it. Dominic grew a lopsided grin and said, "When's the birthday girl getting home?"

James looked out the drive and replied, "Don't look now, but I think I'll go get the Kleenex—here she comes!"

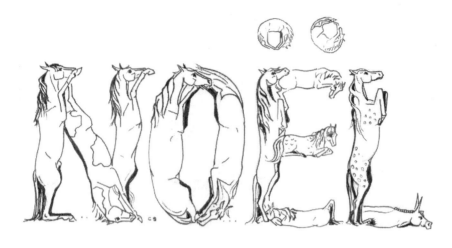

Noel, Noel!

Dots N Dashes called everyone over for a conference.

"All right, listen up, guys. We have to do something special for Ken and Grace this year for Christmas. They look after us all year long and we have to think of something!"

He glanced over to Wally, the pony, whose rotund belly told the story of good feed and plenty of treats.

"Are you paying attention, Wally?" Wally looked up from his steady grazing and managed a contrite look before thrusting his nose back into the tall grass.

"Let's put on a dance!" cried the dainty Arabian mare, and with that, she pirouetted about, flinging lustrous mane and tail this way and that.

"Such a bloody show-off!" grumbled the oldest gelding. "I've got arthritis, and a bad neck!"

"Well, how about a race?" said the elegant but fidgety bay thoroughbred who couldn't stand still.

The short, stocky little paint horse snorted his displeasure at *that* idea, and the two mini horses grimaced and shook their thick shaggy manes in an empathetic and resounding "No!"

"What about we just don't eat for a day? That might save them some money. " said the picky eater of the bunch.

"That's a *terrible* idea!" spouted Wally as his head flew up. "You're such a Thinny Minny!" Thinny Minny was about to snap back when Dots N Dashes called a halt to the quibbling.

"Oh, for Oats Sake, let's get working on something we *all* could do!" The two minis agreed in another tumbled mane "yes!"

With that, the horses and ponies lowered their heads in thought. Some swished their tails, some nipped at a late autumn fly, and others licked their lips in deep concentration. After a time, Noel, the shy standardbred mare, said in the tiniest of voices, "How about a snow message?"

"A WHAT?" bellowed the Percheron. *"Speak up!"* The diminutive mare jumped about a foot in the air, and her breath came in short gasps. "I-I thought, well, I thought that maybe we could...uh, possibly, if we would be able to...like, uh, all lie down—"

She was interrupted once again by the German Warmblood who leaned in toward her. "Vat? Wot are you shpeakink abut?"

"WE COULD SPELL OUT A WORD—LIKE "NOEL!"" she shouted and then shrank back from her audaciousness.

"Lie down? That would be great!" replied the broodmare. "My back is killing me!"

Everyone began to chatter and whinny at once, and the cacophony was ear-shattering.

131

"*Shush!*" yelled Dots N Dashes, with a glance to the house. "They'll think that we're fighting!" "Wouldn't be the first time," one muscular gelding said huskily to another. "Oh, yeah? Bring it on!" came the answer. A wicked glance from their leader had them settled down, however, and they decided to learn more about the NOEL idea because all of them wanted to return to their favorite spots in the pasture.

The standardbred mare stood in the center of all of the horses. She said, "See that nice hill right there in front of the house, by the big window where Ken and Grace have their morning coffee? If we laid ourselves out just right, we could spell a small word…like NOEL. " Her big brown eyes flitted back and forth to see the reaction from her stablemates. Instead of laughing at her, they seemed to embrace the idea, particularly since it was something that everyone could participate in.

"We'd have to practice a bit," said Dots N Dashes thoughtfully. "But it could work! By Christmas, there should be a lot of snow on that hill and it would be like doing horse angels in the snow!" The petite Arab mare sighed and batted her long lashes. "Oh, yes, that would be exquisite!"

With that, most of the horses and ponies went off for their afternoon pleasure while the standardbred mare and Dots N Dashes worked out the details.

They chose a remote part of the pasture to practice. At first, it seemed hopeless.

"Get your hoof off my rump!" "Your tail is in my eyes!" "If you just weren't so clumsy!" And on it went as the horses tried to stretch and bend to make the word "Noel" on the brown, wispy winter grass.

There were fourteen horses and ponies, but only thirteen were needed. No one wanted to be left out. Finally the kind, dappled Shetland pony spoke. "I'll be the one," she said softly. "No, no, no!" cried Dots N Dashes. "You are part of the "E"!

"Oh, I'm an "E"! she said, lifting her tiny head majestically.

Weeks went by and Christmas was but one day away. The practicing had paid off, yet no snow arrived to cover the ground. The horses were very pleased with themselves, but severely disappointed as they looked at the barren hill. They put their great heads together and prayed for snow. It was a special, quiet moment as the horses stood in a circle, tails at rest, eyes closed.

"Dear Lord," said one, "we are grateful for our daily hay, our health, and our strong legs beneath us. "We are thankful for our humans Ken and Grace, who provide us our sustenance and grain and a shelter from the storm. But Lord, we really need a storm. Amen. "

The silence lasted but a few moments, and then was interrupted.

"He nipped me!"
"No, I did *not!*"
"Yes, you did!"
"No, I didn't!"

Dots N Dashes sighed. The prayer meeting was over.

Lo and behold, the skies began to darken and a soft snow began to fall. All of the horses and ponies raced about and flung their tails high to the astonishment of their owners, who watched the spectacle with some degree of uncertainty. "Loco weed?" said Ken. Grace shook her head back and forth in the dizzying, crystalline-like flakes of snow as they began to fall harder. She looked up and smiled, for she knew it was the refreshing December snow that made them run like colts and fillies across the field, now lint-like and pale.

The snow quit early on Christmas morning.

Ken and Grace arose and began their morning routine after a warm Christmas day snuggle. The old coffee pot was perking away as they prepared to sit and have a quick bit of toast and jam before feeding the animals. Grace was first to see. "Oh, no! Call the vet!" she shouted. Ken bustled over and with a slack jaw looked out the window and onto the hill, which was now filled with horses down. Dots N Dashes was the only one standing, as he proudly overlooked his mates from his stance atop the hill, His head was high and he was stock-still, like a statue in the park.

"Wait! Wait!" said Ken. "Look at them! They have spelled out the word "NOEL."

Grace leaned forward and rubbed her eyes. "Why they surely did! It is amazing! It is just amazing!"

Grace and Ken ran to the door and flung it wide. Not one horse spooked as they clapped and woo-hooed at the incredible sight. At long last, heads poked up from the bed of snow and then the horses and ponies stood in a line and bowed their necks. Tears moistened Grace's eyes as she knew that this was one very special Christmas gift that they would never forget. Even Santa would have to agree that he'd been beaten by a mile, and on that beautiful day, the carrots flowed like fine champagne.

The Letter

Dedicated to all our brave men and women in uniform.

November 1

Dear Son,

I hope this letter finds you well and healthy. We miss you terribly, and we pray for your safety every day—I do believe the whole town does! I hope you like the Christmas gifts that I have sent and that the packages arrive in time for Christmas. How strange it must feel to not have a frosty winter's breath, or snow licking at your eyelashes! We have already gotten a fair amount of snow, even this early in November. The horses have thick, rich coats, and they are quite a sight to see as they gallop to the fence for breakfast when Father gets the old Ford tractor gunning. I know you must miss your horses the most, and when I close my eyes, I see you there with them. They miss you, too, I can tell.

I must tell you this now, before word should arrive from elsewhere. Your dear old gelding, Major, has passed on. He was failing the last month or so, and one evening he didn't come in with the rest. We found him lying peacefully where he had collapsed; we know he did not suffer. I hate to give you this news, for he was your treasure. If ever a horse loved a boy, it was he loving you. We buried him high atop the hill and placed a marker there. I'm so sorry. I hope this news won't be too hard to take, I cannot bear to think of you sad so far away from home.

I will close for now. God keep you and bless you.

Mom

Christmas Day

Dear Mom and Dad,

It is Christmas today, and I think of nothing but being home with you. Thank you for all of the great gifts and treats; my buddies are jealous! Some of the guys don't have much of a family, and I share what I can. We're all in this together. Thank you for telling me about Major. I have thought of him much since I got the news, and it has given me many moments when my mind can take me far away from this wretched camp and unfamiliar land of war and death and human suffering. Today I was thinking of all the Christmases when I took Major into town for the parade and dressed him up like a reindeer—remember? And how about the time he tore up the manger scene by the church, rooting around for hay! All those Christmas mornings when I'd run out and try on a new bridle or saddle pad … bury my face in his warm coat … feel his strong back under me when we galloped through the snow. How I wish I could go back to those times, just once more. I'll tell you a little secret now that only Maj and I knew.

There were times when I was a kid that I would make up a note for the teacher and sneak home from school. From the tall weeds up there by the road, I could see Dad in the fields, or you hanging out the wash and little brother playing around the sandpit. I'd whistle softly for Major, and he'd pick up those big old ears and come to me. We'd ride on down to the orchard, way back by the woods, and spend the day together splashing in the creek and riding the back pasture until it was safe to come home! Our favorite place was an apple tree back there, because I could climb it and Major could graze, and we'd share a few apples when we could find them. I sat in that tree when Grandpa died, and I sat in that tree one whole day when my girl broke up with me. Major would hang out and wait for me; I think he would have cried with me if he could have. We took one last ride out there before I left. That's when I said good-bye to him, and we walked home side by side in the cool of the day. I didn't know if I'd ever see him again.

I know I'll not forget that Christmas morning when you put Mom's red scarf over my eyes and sat me in front of the kitchen window. I remember every heart-pounding minute and every second until you took off the blindfold, and I saw Dad with his big smile, holding on to that young colt dancing around in the snow! He was pawing, and prancing, and showing off—well, he won my heart right then and there. My first horse. He sure was a good one, and although he is gone, Major gave me more than anyone will ever know. I'm glad he didn't suffer. Just remembering all of this makes me feel close to home and to all of you. I'll be there soon; don't you worry about me. I'm going to bed now, where I can ride the night away in my dreams—maybe even have a snowball fight or a piece of your famous rhubarb pie! Thanks for everything, and give my horses a good rub for me when you can. Merry Christmas; I love you all so much.

Your son

Day after Christmas

Dear Son,

Sorry to have taped this note on the outside of your care package, but I had already sealed it! I forgot to mention to you that when we found Major he was lying peacefully underneath an old apple tree way in the back by the woods. Maybe you would know which one.

Love, Mom

Cindy Seng has enjoyed a lifetime with horses and is an author of award winning stories. She is also an artist working in oils and bronzes, nearly of of which have an equine theme. She lives with her husband Bill on a Illinois farm where they board and train horses. They spend their free time riding trails near and far, and particularly enjoy their getaway in Marquette, Michigan where they have a cabin and barn for their horses.

Cindy began her horse career with a patient gelding, and soon after bought Texas bred Lady T Jet, a fast quarter mare who led her to many wins for barrel racing at local shows as well as competition in the rodeo arena. In her younger years, she learned to rope and hazed cattle for her bulldogging husband, took English jumping lessons, and did just about anything to learn more about horses and riding. Cindy now takes pleasure in trail riding her gelding Nemo or driving her antique buggy behind a matched team of Welsh Pony mares.

Their three grown children, share their enthusiasm for animals and the outdoors and while growing up always had a safe pony or horse to ride.

Right behind riding horses for Cindy is either painting them, sculpting them, or writing stories about them.

Friends, family and horses have always been a special combination in the Seng household.

"Holidays in particular have always given me many happy moments in life," Cindy notes. "But Christmas is truly my favorite! When the December snow flies, the horses are happy, too. They seem to know it is a special, wonderful season and a fresh start to a new year!"

CPSIA information can be obtained
at www.ICGtesting.com
Printed in the USA
FFOW04n1407150216
21514FF

9 781463 411817